BIRD MEMORIES
OF THE ROCKIES

BOOKS BY ENOS A. MILLS

THE GRIZZLY, OUR GREATEST WILD ANIMAL

YOUR NATIONAL PARKS

THE STORY OF SCOTCH

THE ROCKY MOUNTAIN WONDERLAND

THE STORY OF A THOUSAND-YEAR PINE

IN BEAVER WORLD

WILD LIFE ON THE ROCKIES

THE SPELL OF THE ROCKIES

BIRD MEMORIES OF THE ROCKIES

LONG'S PEAK (14,255 FEET)
Looking across the valley from the homestead cabin

BIRD MEMORIES OF THE ROCKIES

BY
ENOS A. MILLS

WITH ILLUSTRATIONS

BOSTON AND NEW YORK
HOUGHTON MIFFLIN COMPANY
The Riverside Press Cambridge
1931

The Riverside Press
CAMBRIDGE · MASSACHUSETTS
PRINTED IN THE U.S.A.

NOTE

A PART of these chapters has appeared in magazines. Acknowledgment is made to the publishers for permission to reprint this material: *The Saturday Evening Post*, 'The Wit-Cracker Jay' (February 21, 1920), 'The Big American Bird' (May 3, 1919); *The American Boy*, 'Calling on Birds' (July, 1921) and 'The Adventures of a Tree' (May, 1921); *Sunset Magazine*, 'Little Blue' (January, 1924); and *The Estes Park Trail*, 'Enos Mills' (May 23, 1924).

PREFACE

Your winged, cheerful friends the birds are the great bond between nature and humanity. With their human characteristics; their songs, colors, and flight; their courtships, nest-building, and family life; their inquisitiveness, courage, and friendliness; their mysterious migrations, returning year after year to the same locality; birds, intelligently studied, give us sympathy for every living thing.

What realms they have conquered! — all! Birds are at the farthest north with the ice-crags and snow flowers, in riot of tropical vegetation, on deserts where chaos rules, and on the peaks with cañons and clouds. Every land and sea they can claim by the right of discovery and occupancy, and by their ever watching over it and singing to it.

Their recognition of the principle of coöperation is apparent in their instinct to congregate in flocks for migration and in using the advantages of sentinels and leaders. And otherwise they work together for the best interests of the flock. Cranes are known to send out scouts to report before the flock goes; pelicans fish in coöperation; penguins have coöperative day nurseries to keep the active young birds within bounds while the old birds are off food-hunting; jays and robins unite to battle an undesirable neighbor. They sometimes care for the young of other birds left helpless, and befriend the aged of the race.

Their actions show intelligent interest in life and a progressive understanding of their place in it. Many of the traits of head and heart that we have they also have. They give evidence of reason and memory.

One bird-student has said, 'What we know about bird-life bears no comparison to what we do not know.'

Having an opportunity to observe birds in their domestic affairs, to appreciate their actions and antics, hear the songs and notes of mating-time, watch the work of nest-building, of guarding the nest, feeding the babies, bringing up the children, and see the preparations for the southland, has been my good fortune. This intimate acquaintance has given me a bigger conception and infinitely better opinion of birds than I should have believed possible.

The songs, notes, and tones — the language of

birds — are of rare interest. 'Phit,' 'tut,' 'chack,' seem to be common bird words to express surprise, warning, objections to trespass, or all these — and more. But the utterances of birds of the same species are not always alike. Birds, like people, will in unusual times give very different calls and notes from those ordinarily heard. Sometimes, when alone, a mother bird will look down into her cradle and sing strangely, 'soft and low.'

Birds sometimes talk in an undertone, soliloquize, or sing to themselves. There is great individuality in bird music and there are many degrees of excellence in the delivery of the family song. There is often a marked change in the arrangement and variety of bird words; yet we recognize it as the same subject, just as we should recognize two orations on 'The Art of Living' though given by different speakers. Bird-songs vary with individuals, with age, with seasons, conditions, environments, and emotions.

Without the birds how dreary and desolate would be the earth! how sad and lonely the out-of-doors without their bright presence and cheerful songs! A friend has been defined as the first person to come in when the whole world has gone out.

PREFACE

You will ever find the birds young and hopeful, eager to be friends. They are waiting for you.

It is important for the welfare of our race that we give to birds in fullest degree their right to life, liberty, and the pursuit of insects.

ENOS A. MILLS

CONTENTS

INTRODUCTION, BY JOHN T. JACOBS	XV
THE LOVE SONG OF LITTLE BLUE	I
THE INDIVIDUALITY OF BIRDS	33
A GOLDFINCH ROMANCE	53
THE WIT-CRACKER JAY	73
THE PTARMIGAN AT HOME	93
CALLING ON BIRDS	115
A BIRD IN THE BUSH	135
THE ADVENTURES OF A TREE	155
GUARDIANS OF THE FOREST	179
MUSIC OF THE WILDS	197
THE BIG AMERICAN BIRD	213
WITH FAMOUS TRAVELERS	237

ILLUSTRATIONS

LONG'S PEAK	*Frontispiece*
THE HOMESTEAD CABIN IN WINTER	4
WHERE THE BLUEBIRDS NESTED	4
Photograph by Sam Freed	
THE UPPER EDGE OF THE MOUNTAIN FOREST	16
Photograph by Dudley C. Rowe	
BABY MOUNTAIN BLUEBIRDS	30
Photographs by Enos A. Mills and Esther B. Mills	
THE NUTCRACKER	42
Photographs by Esther B. Mills	
ROCKY MOUNTAIN GRAY JAYS	46
Photographs by Esther B. Mills	
AN ASPEN WILD-FLOWER GARDEN	62
Photograph by Frank C. Ervin	
A LONG-CRESTED JAY	76
Photograph by R. A. Gilliam	
LONG-CRESTED JAYS AT FEEDING-TABLE	76
THE SUMMER AND WINTER HOMES OF THE PTARMIGAN AND THE ROSY FINCH ABOVE TIMBER-LINE	96
THE PTARMIGAN IN AUTUMN PLUMAGE	100
Photograph by R. A. Gilliam	
THE PTARMIGAN AT TWELVE THOUSAND FEET	100
THE PTARMIGAN AT HOME IN WINTER WITH SNOW AND SUNSHINE	106
Photograph by Edward R. Warren	
A HIGH PLATEAU IN THE ROCKIES	122
GRAY-HEADED JUNCOS	132
Photographs by R. A. Gilliam	

ILLUSTRATIONS

The Western Nighthawk 144
 Photographs by Olive C. Siverling

An Aspen Grove in the San Juan Mountains of Colorado 160
 Photograph by L. C. McClure

Enos A. Mills Examining Cones in a Timber-Line Tree 164
 Photograph by Esther B. Mills

Spruce in the Winter Woods 174

A Crystal-White Alder 174

Western Yellow Pine 184

Colorado Blue Spruce 184

A Limber Pine that Survived a Forest Fire 194

A Twisted Limber Pine Killed in a Forest Fire 194

An Alpine Lake, a Meeting-Place for Birds 200

Sunset from Above the Timber-Line, when the Solitaire Sings 200

A Baby Water-Ouzel Napping between Feedings 204
 Photograph by Edward R. Warren

A Mountain Chickadee 204
 Photograph by H. L. Standley

A Mountain Lake 220
 Photograph by Esther B. Mills

A Forested Cañon below Timber-Line in the Rockies 240
 Photograph by Dudley C. Rowe

The Broad-Tailed Hummingbird 256
 Photographs by H. L. Standley and P. A. Smoll

Except as otherwise indicated the illustrations are from photographs by Enos A. Mills.

INTRODUCTION

THOSE who live next door to genius, and neighbor with it and know it intimately, rarely recognize it. While the world praises, they see nothing unusual; they see the little faults and say, 'There is nothing extraordinary here.' It was always so.

Enos Mills had the highest degree of individuality of almost any man I ever met. There was nothing about the man or his opinions that was standardized. He formed his own judgments of men and institutions and events, irrespective of what the majority thought. He was intensely original and individual. Such men are extremely rare.

The man began life without means or financial help of any kind. He did not have the great educational advantages of Muir and Thoreau, both of whom were trained in the finest universities of the land. If ever there was a self-made man, it was Enos Mills.

All those who knew him as a boy, all those who knew him as a man, will have to pass on before the world will see him in his true proportion. His intimates, with the few exceptions of those who really knew him, saw his little peculiarities and did not see the man as a whole.

With the universal sight of genius he saw even in boyhood the uniqueness and charm of Estes Park. He located a homestead that he might call some of the land his own. The little claim-shack where he lived in youth still stands. In years to come this cabin will be as much a shrine as the spot where Thoreau's cabin stood on the shores of Walden Pond. Even now there are those who go each season to lay a sprig of evergreen at the door in tribute to his memory.

Few people recognized the terrific energy that burned in Enos Mills — his princely ego, always struggling for self-expression. It was an enormous work that he cut out for himself. Penniless, friendless, burdened with a high-strung nervous system and a marvelous individuality, unique, peculiar among men and little understood, and with but little schooling, he had to begin by educating himself. One thing he had always, at least one fond friend. So, with the help of first one and then another, he began to train himself.

Some nameless friend (but not to me unknown) saw his genius and told him he could write. Even then he spoke well. But could he write? How many times this lonely man must have asked himself this question! It was not so clear at first. There were long waits for decisions on manuscripts. Success did not come in a minute, but it did come. His books have done a vast amount of good.

He acquired the old Lamb ranch, and constructed the lodge called Long's Peak Inn, one of the quaintest, one of the most original inns in the world. It was built for expression of himself, just as he wrote his books. His energy burned within him like an unceasing fire and gave him no rest nor peace. Few people appreciate the time, labor, and ability required to build it. It was Enos Mills — the grounds, the buildings, the great lobby, the fireplaces, the dining-room, the quaint rules which still prevail, the collections of books and flowers, and the uncanny totem-poles from timber-line — all are Enos Mills. He will never lack a monument while this lodge stands. Into this place he threw all his intense energy, all his money, all his fierce craving for self-expression, all his genius and all his sense of the fitting and the proper.

He had a still deeper purpose than self-expression in his writings. His passionate devotion to Estes Park made him wish that people everywhere might know of it. He wrote to awaken their interest, to bring them here, to teach them their first toddling steps in nature as best he could. He was successful in it. He did more to make Estes Park known to the world than all other men combined.

The vision of such men, when accompanied by the ability to carry out their ideals, puts us under a lasting obligation of grateful appreciation.

Genius is only universal sight and universal understanding, coupled with mighty energy. Enos Mills had these qualities.

I first saw him in his youth, later knew him well, entertained him and was entertained by him, walked with him, watched him, and studied him. That he was a genius I haven't the slightest doubt.

Always, when I enter the Park and look to the splintered top of old Long's Peak, I think of him. They are associated together in the minds of men. Estes Park is a little lonelier since he went away. It seems a little empty, there is a feeling of incompleteness, a suggestion of the vacant chair at the banquet-table. It will never be quite the same to those of us who remember.

Down the long, long trails of time the story of Estes Park and Enos Mills will pass together.

JOHN T. JACOBS

THE LOVE SONG OF LITTLE BLUE

BIRD MEMORIES
OF THE ROCKIES

∴

THE LOVE SONG OF LITTLE BLUE

A MOUNTAIN bluebird and his mate arrived at my home one March day, alighting on the pole fence by my uncompleted log-cabin, as though surprised to see me. Perhaps they had been reared in the region, while I was a newcomer. After a moment's pause, Mr. Bluebird flew away to examine a hollow limb in a near-by pine. He looked in and went in, flew back to his mate and then to the tree again, and finally returned and persuaded her to come and examine this possible nesting-site. She went reluctantly, and after a look or two evidently condemned the location. Both resumed their position on the fence, content to rest after their long journey from the Southland.

The bluebird is the confidential messenger of the life-moving season of the year, his cheerful presence assuring us that summer will arrive tomorrow for a long and glorious stay. This was good news to me, a boy of sixteen, anxious to complete my cabin,

3

which I had started the summer before to build by myself.

This pair of bluebirds lingered near day after day. They had leisure and enjoyed it lovingly. They were in no hurry to start nest-building. They were weeks ahead of the birds that migrated farther northward, several thousand miles, to secure the same climatic and food conditions which my birds found here in the mountains. Being day travelers, combining food-hunting with travel, they had covered only a short distance each day on their migratory flight from the South. It is probable that they had had opportunity to do their mating on the way; or they may have nested in these scenes before, possibly even in the near-by pine.

My cabin stood in a grove of pine and aspen on a steep mountain-side, sloping south and west. It was nine thousand feet above sea-level. I had few neighbors, and so was eager to make friends with the wild birds and animals that lived near me. Often, as I stood in the doorway, looking across at Long's Peak, which towered more than five thousand feet above me, the rabbits, squirrels, and chipmunks hopped by unafraid. I moved about quietly, never harmed them, and they soon came to

THE HOMESTEAD CABIN IN WINTER

WHERE THE BLUEBIRDS NESTED

know that they were in a safety zone around my home.

The two bluebirds evidently liked the surroundings and often appeared to be watching the slow building of my cabin. At last, one morning before the front of the house was finished, they took possession. I lived in my cabin that summer without completing it, unwilling to disturb the bluebirds and the building of their nest above the ridgepole. From this nest scores of little girls and boys in blue have looked out upon the world.

I had much opportunity to enjoy bluebird ways and companionship. It was not long before they were accustomed to my watching them, and in a month we were friendly. By September they would come into my cabin, and frequently they lunched with me on my writing-table or one on each shoulder as I stood outdoors near the cabin.

The bluebirds were affectionate and devoted. He was a handsome fellow, cheerful, fearless, and calm through all emergencies. Faithfully he performed his daily duties, and ever was free from curiosity or contempt, appearing to have complete indifference for the rest of the world. His favorite seat was the top pole of the fence, about fifteen feet distant from the nest. Here he sat very erect and motionless, like a philosopher. He was interested in no one's affairs but his own.

His trim, modestly attired little mate did most of the work, assumed all the responsibility, and was just a trifle nervous. Occasionally, indifferent to my nearness, these two sat on the pole fence lovingly, close together — he perfectly perpendicular, though in repose, she restless, facing first one side of the fence, then the other. Once in a while she would pull herself up for a moment of deliberation, or to speak low, loving words to her blue prince. To these terms of endearment the prince listened with greatest interest, though he sat motionless and held himself up like an Indian.

The mountain bluebird is the bluest of the blue. No bird that I know carries a color that more completely matches the turquoise or cerulean blue of mountain skies.

The male is bright blue above and pale blue beneath, while she has an ashen-colored coat, thinly, unevenly washed with blue. The youngsters wear ashen brown; around the throat this is dark, and beneath a pale wash over white. This famous color-bearer displays the blue of the sky throughout the middle mountain zone of all western North America, from central Alaska to central Mexico.

One day, as the pair sat side by side on the fence, a robin alighted on a post only a few yards away, apparently without seeing them. Certainly the robin did not know that he was intruding, and he manifested not the slightest evil intentions. Instantly, however, Mother Bluebird hurled herself at the intruder as though to annihilate him, though she was provokingly small for such a task. The robin, apparently chagrined, and certainly surprised and frightened, made haste to escape. Mrs. Bluebird returned to the pole and edged up close to her mate. While they exchanged conversational twitters, he looked at her tenderly and then made haste to bring her a worm. It was offered with much gallant show and accepted demurely.

Another day, after they had had a few loving moments on the fence, he suddenly unbent and faced her with fluttering wings and worshipful attention. I do not know what had been said, but she becomingly received these attentions with quiet dignity. After another moment of admiration he flew to the nest hurriedly, then back again; went to it a second time, looked in, lingered a moment, and then returned to his mate. After a little more gallantry on his part, they flew away to lunch together.

There were five light-blue eggs laid, and thirteen days later both father and mother worked overtime supplying the crying needs of these helpless mites. I was completely ignored in the busy life of these devoted parents. I found that this was true throughout the bird world. During feeding-time, mid-June and later, I made the acquaintance of other bird families nesting in hollow trees, in bushes and branches, and on the ground around my cabin.

While Mrs. Bluebird was brooding the second nestful of eggs, her blue prince took the first brood in hand; patiently he fed and trained them after the ways considered good by bluebirds. These youngsters saw but little of their mother for three weeks after they left the nest, but almost constantly followed their busy father about.

When the second brood hatched, these children were early on hand to see the babies, and, as soon as allowed, they carried them food. Three of the grown-up children worked faithfully in food-hunting and in feeding the nestful of babies, and apparently they did their task well, for Mother Bluebird stayed close by, supervising or serenely looking on. One of the sisters often lingered by the nest after bringing food, watching them with lively curiosity and almost maternal interest.

The two broods of children and their parents lingered around my cabin till late summer, instead of flying farther up the mountain-side, as did so many families, to feed and frolic around timber-line. But autumn appeared to make them uneasy. They knew they must start for the southland before the coming of the cold days.

One glorious September day they joined a flock of bluebirds passing through. Here and there some golden leaves still shone on the aspens; occasionally there was a whisper from the air and the pines. I had marked the old birds, and as they flew away with their two broods of children, I called out: 'Come back early next spring. I'll be looking for you. And be sure to bring those copper threads I have placed around your ankles.'

Many birds mate for life and return to the same locality year after year. Food scarcity, increased dangers, or better opportunities may cause them sometimes, like people, to go to a better, new home.

These bluebirds returned the next spring, and the two following. They lived around my cabin for four successive summers. They had found it a good place in which to bring up their children.

The first bluebirds to arrive near my cabin reported about the first week of March. But these bluebirds were bound farther north. My birds rarely arrived earlier than the 25th of March. This was a month in advance of nesting — a month for relaxation and picnicking. Commonly after arrival they remained in the region, though they sometimes disappeared for two or three days. A late spring snow always sent them out of the storm zone where food could still be obtained on the wing.

I was glad to have my bluebirds over the ridge log again. These cheerful, loving mates had two broods each summer and raised thirty-three children in three years. After all the care that these children had required, they began housekeeping the fourth season as eagerly and as lovingly as though it was the first time.

The nest used three previous summers was renovated and partly rebuilt according to the latest models. From this summer residence and nursery little girls and little boys in blue again looked out with wondering interest upon the strange, big world while their wings were growing.

I had little opportunity during the fourth summer of our friendship to watch over Mr. and Mrs. Bluebird. But it was a joy to see them each day, and to know that they were safe. They had chosen one of the best of places for their family, and I could not imagine anything bringing them harm.

Early one June morning I left my cabin for a day by the timber-line. The bluebirds sat on the fence by the gate. I bade them good-bye and touched them with my hand. We were old friends. They seemed to watch me as I went on up the mountain.

During my absence a boy from a tourist camp near by visited my cabin. He was enthusiastic over barbaric sport, to which he had been reared. Having heard nothing of wild-life conservation, and having nothing else to do, he amused himself by shooting at the bluebirds. They, together with other birds, squirrels, chipmunks, and rabbits around my cabin had learned to trust man. The fearless mother and father bluebirds allowed him to come close. Regardless of the fact that they were tame, he shot one, then the other, and carried the mangled birds to camp to recount his feat to proud parents.

Even with isolation and watchfulness, the fatal day had come to this little bluebird home beneath the end of my cabin ridge log. Returning home after dark that night, I realized that the bluebirds had been betrayed. In vain five speckled-bibbed babies opened wide their mouths for food; in vain these hungry, forlorn bird children cried and called for their parents.

I carried the nest into my cabin. Here was I, a bachelor, with a family to bring up! Fate had given me five hungry, poorly dressed orphans, and I was to be both mother and father to them.

One little fellow died the first day. A week later, while they were huddled on the floor together, a merry chipmunk tipped a book off the shelf, crushing another. The remaining three came to depend upon me for everything. I tried to understand the youngsters and to care for them according to their needs.

After the first week I put the babies to bed in an old hat on the bookshelf. A handkerchief was spread over them, and three or four towels piled on top to keep them from climbing or tumbling out of bed. Later they had the freedom of the cabin floor during the daytime and were allowed to spend their nights where they pleased. Generally they went to sleep cuddled together in the corner.

I can never know how much or how deeply this tragedy influenced and colored my life. I had planned simply to enjoy seeing the parents feed and train these children for their brief and busy existence. Then came the sad event that changed the even tenor of passing days and asked me to be far more than I had ever been and different than I had ever dreamed of being.

It was fortunate for me, and also for these little orphans, that I had watched their mother and father feed, train, and raise a number of bluebird families. The old birds were my first wild-life acquaintance, and I had entered into their daily manners and customs.

I already knew that young birds, like young boys, were always hungry. But, although I worked constantly, apparently there was no filling them up. For a time each of these birds must daily have eaten its weight in combinations of worms, crumbs, grubs, flies, and grasshoppers. They compelled me to work for them, rain or shine. But they developed on the diet supplied, and slowly their speckled bibs and baby clothes were replaced by those for which the bluebird is known.

My bluebirds learned to walk long before they learned to fly. At first they toddled along with most amusing and tumbly short steps. They did much more walking perhaps in this one summer than the average bluebird does in a lifetime. But rarely did they venture far without me, although during the daytime the door was usually open.

Occasionally they came out to me as I sat on the doorstep, and lolled about on the grass and gravel in the sunshine. One sometimes lay down with both legs and wings outstretched. Or one would slowly spread first one wing, then the other; then daintily in turn stretch its legs. For minutes while arranging feathers and enjoying stretching exercises they were unmindful of all else.

Sometimes in the midst of their exercises a chipmunk came along. They would pause a few seconds to look at him, whether from fear or curiosity I could not tell, then continue what they were doing, even though he lingered near. Their parents had not tolerated the chipmunks until their second season was well advanced. If the old birds met a chipmunk in the cabin, or one came close to the door, they promptly assailed the striped visitor, battering him with bill and wings, and sent him scampering. If thoughtlessly a chipmunk climbed up the front of the cabin toward the sacred nest, he was routed. But the young birds finally learned that at least these chipmunks were harmless. They would sometimes sit quietly in one hand while the chipmunks ate from the other.

The day I took the little bluebirds out for their first long walk they were excited, puzzled, and happy. They kept together, close at my heels. Apparently they looked neither to the right nor to the left except when I stopped. We went below to the brook, about one hundred feet down the trail. The movement and the splash of the water aroused curious looks. Then they scattered. But when I called, saying, 'Let's go back,' they hastened to start and made every effort to keep up with me.

15

There were times when I had to shut the children in the cabin and go away for the day. They understood the early morning preparations which preceded a day's absence. I left a little food and plenty of water, but this long shut-in period without any one to play with them they plainly did not like. During these preparations they walked soberly about and did but little else than watch me until I left. How merrily they greeted me on my return, forgetting even hunger for a time in their gladness!

One day, when I was away, a friend of mine called at the cabin. The lonesome little birds were apparently glad to have a caller. But they did not offer to play with him. They received him politely, but without demonstration.

It was different the day a loud-voiced man came into the cabin. Before he had finished the first sentence the birds scampered away and hid behind the wood-box. In fact it was several minutes after he had gone and the room had become quiet again, before they would come out. Then they came ever so cautiously, looking and listening for the first sign of danger.

One day a mother wren who had a nest in a

16

THE UPPER EDGE OF THE MOUNTAIN FOREST

near-by hollow tree, chanced to light in front of the door. Seeing the little bluebirds inside, she ventured in, too. I was seated on the floor, and the bluebirds were scampering around me. Wrens are trustful little birds, but rarely are they curious. But her curiosity was deeply aroused; she was interested almost to excitement, as she stood watching the bluebirds and myself. When one of them alighted on my head, she leaned back on her upturned tail with every attitude and expression of amazement.

Sometimes a young bluebird insists on coming off the nest before the mother is ready, but more often the mother has to encourage and persuade the youngsters to try their wings in flight the first time.

My little bluebirds did not learn to fly in the regular way, nor at the regular time. One day I had placed them on the pole fence, when I happened to notice a gentian, and stooped to look at it, then at another and another near by. I do not know whether I forgot them too long, or if they became curious. Their wings were well grown, but with the exception of stretching exercises, had not been used. They evidently felt this was the opportunity to try them.

As I looked up, one little bird pitched forward and aimed straight for my head with a rapid beating of wings. He went over me and tumbled with an awkward roll on the grass. The other two followed close upon the first, one going some yards beyond him and the other falling short. After this flying experiment they flew about when there was need of it, and sometimes when there was not.

These youngsters, like all children, being intensely interested in food, were generally clamorous if the demand was not promptly supplied. Hunger was so insistent with them that they never forgot it nor allowed me to forget it long at a time. They quickly learned that when I went outdoors with the shovel a supply of grubs would naturally be forthcoming. Then they began following me whenever I picked up the shovel.

One day, shovel in hand, I went up the mountain-side to uproot and transplant an attractive cluster of kinnikinnick. The little birds were not in mind, in fact they were almost independent of me now. But while digging I chanced to look back and discovered that they were coming after me with all their might.

They stood three abreast waiting for something to appear as I dug into the earth by a log. When I turned up a grub or worm, all three seized it at once. But after a tug or two, and without any squabbling, two let go and the other took the prize. I never saw these children disagree; their manners were always perfect. With other birds, too, they acted quietly and with thoughtful consideration, and among themselves there was no trouble. I never saw a quarrel in the family.

A pair of Rocky Mountain gray jays, 'camp-birds,' called on me one day. Of all birds they are the most easily tamed, seeming to enjoy the companionship of man. One lighted on my head and the other on my shoulder as I stood in front of the cabin. The little bluebirds were just walking out of the door. They showed no alarm at the arrival of these big birds, but were greatly interested in seeing them eat from my hand. One of the gray jays occasionally flew to the fence, then back to my head or shoulder. The bluebirds stood still, moving only their heads to follow these flights with their eyes. When the camp-birds finally flew off, the little bluebirds came out and went about their affairs as usual.

19

If they had any feeling of jealousy or antipathy toward these callers, they did not show it.

On another occasion we had a most interesting visit from a bluebird, one who probably was a relative. All four of us were sitting on the fence, when this stranger alighted on the top pole just beyond the farthest bird. After a few seconds he fluttered up to where the nest had been, under the edge of the ridge log, and then back to the fence again. Soon followed a purr-like chatter between the stranger and these three little birds. I felt certain he must be an older brother, born under the end of the ridge log a year or two before. Just before he left I noticed six young bluebirds shyly peeping at us from a near-by tree. They were the same age as my birds. Our visitor flew to them, and from their actions I judged he was their father. From what I saw afterwards he was caring for the first brood of the season while his mate hatched the second nestful of eggs. Their home was in an old wood-pecker hole in a pine a short distance from the cabin.

Though the three little bluebirds and I became

intimately acquainted, only one was named. He was the smallest, the brightest-colored, and always the most alert of the three. I called him 'Little Blue.' He came to me most frequently, and I unconsciously gave him more attention than the other two.

Kittens and puppies, I knew, played and played. When I realized that baby bluebirds, too, would play intently through all their young days, I tried to make Nature's great way as pleasant and as beneficial as possible by providing playthings.

An envelope was hung by a string from the ridge log so that it just cleared the floor, and this was daily enjoyed. Occasionally all tugged at it at once from different directions; sometimes all stood by to watch it dance, swing, and whirl after one had jostled or pulled or struck it.

A hollow, bright-striped rubber ball gave them hours of eager activity. They rolled it about, racing after it and following it all over the floor. When I dropped it, they stood still, watching it curiously as it bounced up and down. When I rolled it against the wall and it came back to them, they dodged and scampered about, pretending to be frightened. A box of shavings afforded them many a mysterious delight. When all played together in it, trampling and plowing through the shavings, they showed as much excited earnestness as children do when playing bear.

Most youngsters like to make a noise, and I found that even gentle, quiet young bluebirds are no exception. One day when in a hurry I placed a tin pan containing a handful of dry beans on the floor. In a moment three children were in the pan stamping about, having a rattling good time. Many a time afterwards when too busy to play with them I took down the tin basin and its ration of dry beans.

They always enjoyed sitting on the pole fence, but expected me to be near them. I was talking to them one day as they sat there, when two little girls and their mother called. It was probably the closest that the children had ever come to bird-life, and it certainly was the first meeting of these bird children with human children. For some seconds the birds looked down, gladly but somewhat bashfully, the little girls looking up with quiet eagerness, hoping to be allowed to touch them. When the little birds were cuddled and talked to in turn, they received it as a matter of course, but appeared happier to be back on the pole fence again.

All three of these blue children were at different times greatly interested in different things, but to the very end of the summer my writing-table never ceased to fascinate Little Blue. It was for him a real fairy place, and he insisted on playing there much of the time.

Generally he entertained himself quietly, but occasionally he indulged in vigorous pranks. Seizing the end of a pencil or penholder in his bill, he backed off to the edge of the table and dropped or pushed it overboard. Then he peered after it, listening with tilted head for it to strike the floor. Each time the rattle made him leap for joy or look up at me with an expression of happy satisfaction. Then he made haste to find something else to throw overboard.

While Little Blue was one day busy on the table, the other two birds went outdoors. The door presently blew shut. Bye and bye Little Blue flew to the floor. Not seeing the other birds, he gave a puzzled chirp and began exploring every corner of the room. Greatly mystified, he stood in the center of the floor for several seconds, listening and apparently thinking. Then slowly, seriously, he began looking for them again. His attitude was one of responsibility. He appeared worried about them rather than lonesome. I opened the door, and out he rushed. Curiously and with grave concern he looked them over, then quickly dismissed his fears when he discovered that they were all right.

Sometimes, while I was writing, Little Blue made it too lively for me. Partly to divert him, I began keeping a covered tin box of crumbs on the table. Often, when he wanted something to eat, he hovered with beating wings just above the box until I opened it. On one occasion he found the box uncovered. Alighting on its edge, he bent forward and peered in, and then looked up at me. The box was empty. He wiped his bill on the edge a time or two and looked at me again. I pretended not to have noticed either him or the empty box. He then clutched the edge of the box in his claws and hammered the table vigorously with it.

One morning, while making merry on the table, he overturned a quart bottle of ink. It fell smash on the floor, and after it tumbled the tin crumb-box. Little Blue, in happiest mood, looked down from the edge of the table, while I gathered up the pieces of the broken bottle. I saved a little of the ink, a scarce article in my part of the world, pouring this into the empty tin box until I could find something better. This gave Little Blue an idea!

Usually each morning the little birds had the opportunity for a bath. Watching the splashy enthusiasm of robins in the brook had suggested to me that the bluebirds might like to try it. They did. But on this particular morning they had not yet been given the opportunity, and Little Blue evidently thought it was time. Just as I returned with an empty bottle he squatted in the tin box and began splashing ink with his wings. I almost drowned him in the water bucket before putting him out in the sun to dry.

Little Blue so greatly confused things in his intense enjoyment of the table that I sometimes covered it when I left the cabin. If I put on my hat, took up the water-bucket, or made other unmistakable preparations to go out, he instantly watched to see whether or not the table would be covered. If not, and I was slow to go after making preparations, he became excited. It was so much in his mind that the instant I was outdoors he pounced upon the table and at once made all haste to clear it off completely.

One day the table was uncovered and he playing with the other birds in the shavings on the floor, when I rose and put on my hat. He at once ceased playing and flew to the back of the chair by the table. I started for the door, with him watching my every move. But on reaching the door I stopped, picked up a pamphlet, and with my back toward him pretended to read. I was watching him closely in the looking-glass. He was all eagerness and excitement at my delay. He stood watching me for a moment, and then the situation appeared to dawn on him — that I could not see him.

Anyway, he stretched his neck, looked the table over, and then took a glance at me. Then he hopped over upon the table. I made no move, and after turning for another look at me, he proceeded to enjoy himself.

Toward the close of summer I kept the table covered when not in use. For this purpose I used a burlap cloth that was barely large enough. Little Blue found a way to uncover it. He one day alighted on a corner of the table and looked at me; then, reaching over and catching the edge of the cover in his bill, he lifted it, tilted his head, and tried to peep under it. Then he let it drop and again looked up at me. As with many a mother, the child triumphed.

Dry climate one day gave him a surprise. He alighted on my shoulder and then hopped upon my head. The weather was extra dry and my crowded, curly hair electrical. Apparently the soles of his feet were strangely tickled. He tried standing on one foot like a stork. Then he tried the other foot. He changed places and feet repeatedly, and finally squatted down in my hair.

I was writing, and on reaching the end of a line I asked, 'Little Blue, can you read that?' Leaning forward and downward, he stared closely at the writing as though trying to understand it.

I frequently talked to the birds in a natural, conversational way, apparently to their great enjoyment. I always talked about something definite, told stories or endeavored to speak sympathetically as though talking to a child. I avoided detached words and meaningless chatter. Often I have won the attention and sometimes the affection of an animal or bird simply by talking calmly, kindly to it.

Little Blue was simply charmed when I did this, especially when I addressed myself to him alone. He sometimes lighted on my table, I think, for the purpose of having me talk to him. I spoke slowly, gently, and cheerfully. After the first few words he looked up into my face and stopped all activities, listening to the end with perfect attention. I sometimes explained to him the ways of other birds, spoke of birds he would meet in the South during the winter. Often I talked to him about his parents, and the ways of bluebirds I had known. Many times he listened with the greatest interest for minutes. But his was almost a silent attention. The bluebird as a species has few chirps, peeps, or calls; it is mostly silent.

One morning I paused in my writing to talk to Little Blue. Pen in hand stood by the last word written. After listening with his usual eagerness, he hopped upon my hand and looked up wonderingly into my face. I continued talking quietly and earnestly. Suddenly, with half-opened and fluttering wings, he began a low, sweet, whispered warble — the love song of the bluebird — all the while looking intensely at me with almost passionate interest. It continued for a little less than a half minute.

This was a dear experience to have with a dumb friend, and it was deep enough for tears.

The day before the birds were called South, I had been talking to Little Blue on the table, when he again sang the whispered warble — I suppose the love song of his heart for his mate.

During early autumn the little bluebirds were uneasy and restless. Evidently they were ready to be off for the southland and to take the great migration journey.

The call came to them when all four of us were sitting close together on the top pole of the fence one still, sunny, thoughtful September morning. I was wondering what the winter had in store for them, for I felt that their migratory instinct would be irresistible. I said: 'Some day you will start on a long and wonderful journey which will carry you over rivers, hills, and fields into the warm southland. Your bluebird companions will travel slowly, in flocks, picnicking on the way. You will have new things to eat in every country where you stop. Before Thanksgiving you should be in central Mexico, or, if you do not go to Mexico you will be in Texas. Wherever you are, you will find thousands of bluebirds, perhaps millions of robins, and hundreds of other species of birds. But bluebirds make short stays in the southland, and long before our winter is over, you will be starting slowly northward. Bluebirds often pass here by the first of March and sometimes rest for a day or two before going on farther. I hope I shall see you next spring; perhaps some of you will stay and nest with me again.'

Suddenly, the plaintive, stirring call of a bluebird was heard. Then several bluebirds alighted on a pole in the next panel of the fence. Leaving my birds interested in the visiting travelers, I backed away to watch them from my cabin. Here and there golden leaves shone on the aspen, and occasionally the serene air of autumn whispered in the pines.

I stood in the doorway watching, and wondering if these three little birds whom I had raised would fly away and leave me. For a time there was an exchange of conversational twitterings and

BABY MOUNTAIN BLUEBIRDS, PERHAPS DESCENDANTS OF LITTLE BLUE

warblings. Then, the far, far-away, mysterious and irresistible migration instinct called, I suppose. True to this, all presently took wing and started south.

But Little Blue circled from the flock and came back to me as I stood in the cabin door. On beating wings he paused in the air just before me, looked at me intently a few seconds, then flew away over the pine grove toward the south after the flock. I felt certain that next spring he would return with a mate to nest beneath my cabin ridge log.

Early in the autumn many local bluebirds ascend the mountains to about twelve thousand feet and sometimes spend two or three weeks along the timber-line. Here they feed on insects and late berries. This autumn in the heights I saw a number of small bluebird flocks of from eight to fifteen, perhaps they were families. I looked and called repeatedly for Little Blue, but there was no response. One day, however, I felt certain that I saw his older brother, the bird who had called upon us, but whose six bashful children remained in the near-by pine.

A few days after the little bluebirds flew away

I left my cabin for a winter in Montana and the Northwest, and I did not return until early the following July. On arrival I paused just long enough to see that there was a nest of baby bluebirds in the old place, then hurried in to examine some papers. Leaving the cabin door open, I took a seat at the table. Suddenly there was a flutter of wings, and a bird alighted on my shoulder, then on the table. He was looking up into my face with worshipful satisfaction.

'Are you Little Blue?' I asked. 'Are those your babies in the nest?'

The answer was the low, sweet, whispered warble — the bluebird's song of love and memory.

THE INDIVIDUALITY OF BIRDS

THE INDIVIDUALITY OF BIRDS

ONE rainy day I was in the top of a tall pine, playing detective and trying to find out what devilish scheme a magpie was up to, when in my eagerness I lost my hold on the slippery limb and fell violently to the ground. My hat fell off as I slipped and lodged upside down in the fork of a high limb.

My fall left me stunned and one leg badly injured, so that I lay on the ground beneath the tree for some hours. A disturbance above finally roused me to look up and see what was the cause of it. It was springtime and robins were about. As usual, they made a great ado and flew here and there, all a-flutter and important, with much exclaiming and consultation.

Two robins were inspecting my hat. After curious discussion they appeared to be about to take up housekeeping in it. Evidently they considered this a gift of the gods. I was unable to recover the hat, and when I left the scene they were in possession. Later in the season I returned more than once to get acquainted with the five

35

little babies that were reared in this unusual nest. Would they consider a hat a prerequisite for nest-building, I wondered.

But birds are progressive. The nests of the same family differ widely. Yet each species seems to have certain requirements to satisfy its individuality. A robin insists on having a tree entirely to himself for his home, while herons sometimes colonize one tree with sixty crowding nests.

Birds spend much time in choosing a suitable nesting-site. They seem to investigate every possibility before making a selection. Perhaps they enjoy this exploring before beginning the strenuous work of nest-building. A woodpecker I watched took eleven days to chisel out a wooden nest; a kingfisher with a football growth of feathers on his head bored a tunnel nest in the bank of the brook in twelve days; a wren by my cabin worked busily to complete her nest in eight, and once a robin spent fifteen days in nest-building.

A pair of kingbirds returned to the elm where they had nested a number of years. But during that winter a wind-storm had taken away the limb on which the nest had been. They seemed unable to believe that the undreamed-of had happened, and flew about in a noisy manner for days. They investigated all the other elms near by, but after much discussion chose a site in the same tree in as near the location of the previous nest as possible.

Penguins near the South Pole make nests of pebbles on the rocks, there being no other nesting-material. When the young ones are large enough to move, they take to the sea, where they feed mostly on shrimps. For winter they go only a few hundred miles, or even less, and live on ice-floes in the sea northward. These birds have lost ability to fly, but are excellent swimmers and fair walkers. In walking, when they are seen in the distance, they appear somewhat like dressed-up little people moving with short steps and a straight, stiff back.

In house-building birds are at least as varied as the various races of people of the earth. There are weavers, masons, carpenters, and birds that make no nest — lay their eggs on the bare ground, like the nighthawk. But the majority of birds build a nest, using sticks, straws, leaves, grass, and moss, and lining it with thistle-down, spider-webs, or feathers. They are located in the greatest variety of places — on the ground, in bushes, on the limbs or forks of trees, and in the very tree-tops.

The woodpecker family seem to go to the most work in the construction of a house of any of our common birds. If a hollow tree is not available, the woodpecker uses its chisel-like bill to excavate a hole. It seems to prefer a dead or soft-grained tree, and the aspen is a great favorite. These woodpecker holes are often taken the following summer by wrens, bluebirds, chickadees, and nuthatches. You can help supply the need which they seem to feel for a wooden-walled house by putting up bird-houses of your own construction.

The swallow family vary much with the species, and with the individual. Some burrow into banks, others make plastered mud and straw nests against cliffs or in caves, while many seek out holes under the eaves of buildings.

The variety of nesting-sites is so great, and each nest is so perfect of its kind, that there would seem to have been architects to set the styles. As with humans, the lady usually selects the site and does most of the house-furnishing. He stays around and gives his approval.

Where conditions are favorable, friendly birds come close to human habitations to nest. This may be for better food opportunities, or for increased safety from enemies, but it is also plain that many of them come to satisfy their desire for human society. Even shy, well-fed birds hope and wait for friendly advances on our part. Most wild life is wild from necessity and not from desire. It is not difficult to see birds at short range. Sit or stand quietly, and if you are interested they will often shorten the distance. Many birds exhibit great curiosity and eagerly investigate the new or the unusual.

Many species of birds mate for life. Two bluebirds who had nested near my cabin lingered for weeks after other bluebirds had gone to the southland. Mrs. Bluebird was nursing a broken wing. I do not know how this happened. But she was regularly fed by Mr. Bluebird. She spent most of the time sitting quietly on a dead limb of the tree in which they had nested. Winter came, and the wing, though apparently healed, was useless. During a prolonged snowstorm he twice tried to find food for her, but both finally perished. Another bluebird that lost its mate spent two summers without a mate. Eagles and some species of woodpeckers mate for life, and the little screech owl has loving loyalty for its mate.

Birds have many of the same instincts and traits that humans have, and just as much individuality. A recognition of this fact will make acquaintance more intimate. They love and hate, are cruel and kind, have anger and jealousy, have sympathy and grief, are curious and courageous, are devoted and loyal.

The magpie is by far the worst bird I know. To give the devil his dues, he does perform a little useful service as a scavenger, but he is a heartless wretch at best. He will steal a baby bird out of another bird's nest and devour it; he will steal the other bird's eggs. And let a poor horse or cow become injured or helpless, and the magpie delights to feed upon the wound it has received and is in glee to be able to eat out its eyes.

On the wild world's stage many an unexpected scene is enacted but once. The unexpected happened one morning on the mountain-side behind my cabin. Two robins set up a great ado as I was approaching a lone pine. Robins so often predict the end of the world or something else that never happens, that I paid no heed to them until they darted at me with angry chatter. Unable from the ground to see the cause of the demonstration, I started to climb the pine. The robins objected and darted about denouncing me vigorously. There on a large limb sat an aged and helpless old jay. His feathers were disarranged, beak and claws worn and blunt, and both eyes blind. Ancestral feuds and recent fights were forgotten. These robins fed the old jay until he tumbled lifeless from his last retreat.

On two occasions I saw male robins feeding young bluebirds. Whether these robins were without young of their own, or simply doing double parental duty, I cannot say.

Most bird species are unfriendly to those of other species. But I do not think that this is true with the young of another species, except with a few, as the magpie, that plunder nests.

As with races of people, there are white birds, red birds, black birds, and brown birds. And in their talk, their habits, their manners, and their dress, their 'make-up,' there is a striking contrast, as with different people.

Many birds are graceful and dignified, others

awkward and ill-mannered. Some always appear well groomed and well dressed, while a few seem to have adopted a freakish fashion and never to have changed. What a variety of feathers and colors nature has bestowed — even to top-knots, epaulettes, and flowing trains!

The cedar waxwings are noted for their gentleness and good manners. They travel in flocks and never seem in a hurry to eat or feed; each appears to be politely waiting for the rest to partake first. They talk together in low tones, keeping up a continual whispering among the entire flock. They are perfectly dressed, in the best of taste, and always well-groomed.

The waxwings and the crossbills are the gypsies of the bird world. They arrive unexpectedly and depart without ceremony. They have no regard for migration-routes or seasons. They undoubtedly follow the food-supply, their own special varieties. But they have no home territory.

How different the ptarmigan and the penguins! The ptarmigan stays in a restricted range, and makes little use of the power of flight. He keeps to his mountain-tops and here is at home to many species of migrating birds. The penguin has lost

THE NUTCRACKER

the use of its wings but has developed a most unique home and community life in the great Antarctic.

In the bird world the male generally wears the gay clothes. Where the male birds wear the plain clothes and the females the pretty ones, it is the male usually who does the work. The northern phalarope is an illustration of this. But other birds are identical in plumage for male and female, as in the crows, jays, and magpies.

In the bird world are many specialists. There are good swimmers, good flyers, and good runners; good talkers, good singers, and good actors. Even among birds of the same kind there is a marked display of individuality; no two robins sing exactly alike, no two flickers build identical nests.

In disposition birds display many human characteristics. There are those that like to appear in the public eye, those that enjoy being with the crowd and making a noise, and those that are always found in quiet places leading the simple life. There are those with composure, and others ever nervous.

The Clark crow, or nutcracker, is boisterous, active, and noisy. Often, when pine nuts are ripe, he is a trouble-maker. He takes delight in assailing a squirrel so vigorously that the cone is dropped. When in safe retreat, the squirrel replies with prolonged and terrific language.

One day, near where I was watching, a nutcracker started a fight between two robins, just how I did not see. But the noise of these robins attracted other robins and many more birds besides. All flew and darted about, shrieking and scolding. It was a riot. Two other nutcrackers, shouting wildly, flew around. The one that had started this disturbance darted about in happy excitement, urging things on. It was some satisfaction when suddenly, in the midst of this, he collided with a tree limb and knocked himself senseless. The crows and jays, however, are among the wisest of birds.

While the nutcracker's pranks lack the subtlety of the crested jay's, he adds much of interest to our Western mountains. He makes a picturesque appearance in his gray and black and white dress, and is never afraid to make himself heard, whether singly or in flocks. His raucous calls, as he picks out the seeds from the pine cones at timber-line, are evidence of his enjoyment of the autumn days and seed harvest. Winter and summer he lives in the upper forests, sometimes soaring to the highest peaks, or descending with spectacular flight into the mountain valleys.

Blue jays are often the policemen-sentinels of the woods — to warn the rest of the world of an invader. But the long-crested jay is a bureau-crat; he has ability, brains, eyes, ears, agility, courage of a kind; but he must rule or ruin. A part of the time he can be credited with devoting to uplifting, and ruling with the feeling that benevolent despotism is a good thing, but he wants to boss everybody.

In strong contrast is the Rocky Mountain gray jay, or 'camp-robber,' who is almost a silent woodsman. Quiet, gentle, and confiding, he is the perfect companion of the trail or camp-fire; never intruding, yet ever expecting and accepting a portion of the fare. They, also, are permanent residents of the upper forest, keeping more in it and less in the open. They will discover any unusual food-supply, around habitations or else-where, caching this for future consumption.

When alone in 'the twilight of the forest noon' that sweet singer, the hermit thrush, literally puts his woods into song. He gladdens the mellow-lighted forest aisles, and tells of the mystery, the romance, and the sublimity of the solitudes. The water-ouzel is never of the crowd, but haunts his chosen stream, mingling his liquid melody with wild cascades. The owl, too, is a lover of reserve and philosophic reflection. You will always find him in the silent places.

I ever associate chickadees and children — their perpetual motion, cheerfulness, slightly disarrange'¹ clothes, and continual merry chatter — they are so busy, so exceedingly merry. Life seems to be one constant round of attention to the necessary duties and pleasures of living. And even if it is ever so cold and even rainy and windy, the day is never so dull or uncomfortable that it makes them forget to sing.

The little house wren is a bird of extraordinary vitality. It is exceedingly active and appears to be eternally on the move. It has never learned repose. It is jumping and hopping and flitting and bowing and scolding all day long. I have never been able to understand how such a nervous, fidgety little being enjoys living so closely associated with nervous human beings. It uses a part

ROCKY MOUNTAIN GRAY JAYS

of its surplus energy by carrying excessive quantities of sticks for its exceedingly small nest. And when it sings it does so with intense enthusiasm and with a force that causes its small body to vibrate. Ofttimes I have heard two rival wrens singing each with all its might, repeating their individual songs over and over again, several times a minute.

It would be interesting to know why the European wren sometimes builds two or even three nests that are complete except furnishings and never uses but one of them.

And what characteristic or peculiarity of the gull is it that accounts for its never eating dead birds on land and yet quickly devouring them when thrown into the sea?

Birds give every evidence of reason and memory. It is so common as to be a well-established fact, that birds return year after year to the same locality to nest. How they find their way is still one of the unexplained factors in bird life, but memory is undoubtedly the predominating trait that enables them to do this.

Birds unite against a temporarily triumphant enemy or coöperate to battle a hawk or other undesirable fellow in feathers that invades the locality.

A clamor of many kinds of birds one morning called me into a near-by grove. There on a limb sat an owl, chagrined and annoyed at the consternation and clamor of a whole mixed flock of birds. They were keeping up a constant disorder of noisy name-calling. He left the neighborhood in disgust, and was conducted away by an agitated mob of excited resident robins.

One day a hawk made a dash for a dove, missed, and lighted in a tree on the edge of this grove. He was seen by a robin, whose alarm cries brought the surrounding bird population to the scene. While the hawk, noticing the confusion, was probably watching an opportunity to escape, he was struck by a jay that had darted in unseen. As the hawk flew off, the jay battered him vigorously, a few flying feathers showing the hawk was having the worst of it. All the way back to the grove the jay shouted his triumph.

In 'The American Beaver' Morgan cites the following interesting instance of mutual aid:

'Captain Stansbury gives the following account of a blind pelican upon one of the islands of the

Great Salt Lake of Utah. "In a ramble around the shores of the Island, I came across a venerable looking old pelican, very large and fat, which allowed me to approach him without attempting to escape. Surprised at this apparent tameness, we examined him more closely, and found that it was owing to his being entirely blind, for he proved to be very pugnacious, snapping freely, but vaguely, on each side, in search of his enemies, whom he could hear but could not see. As he was totally helpless, he must have subsisted on the charity of his neighbors, and his sleek and comfortable condition showed, that like beggars in more civilized communities, he had 'fared sumptuously every day.' The food of these birds consists entirely of fish, which they must necessarily obtain from Bear River, from the Weber, the Jordan, or from the Warm Springs on the eastern side of Spring Valley, at all of which places they were observed fishing for food. The nearest of these points was more than thirty miles distant, making necessary a flight of at least sixty miles to procure and transport food for the subsistence of their young.'"

Stansbury also writes, 'Immense numbers of

young birds were huddled together in groups about the island, under the charge of a grave looking nurse or keeper, who, all the time that we were there, was relieved from guard at intervals as regularly as a sentinel.'

Birds have their troubles and tragedies, their hopes and their joys. They travel and play, both singly and collectively; they gossip and pry into the personal affairs of others. They have social life, dances, and community gatherings. They unite for the common welfare. Their manners and customs, their home life, their courtships, their house-hunting and home-building, their ways of teaching their children, their adventures and their strange migrations, all give them an interest — a higher value — for us.

Birds rank with the fine arts — music, poetry, painting, and literature — in revealing to us the beauty and the joy of existence. They add much to childhood; they cheer, interest, and arouse thought, by telling a part of an ever-continued story, by compelling pleasant concentration, and by appealing to the imagination and to the sympathies.

If my island in the sea could have but four

kinds of birds, I should choose the chickadee, the goldfinch, the water-ouzel, and the solitaire. They are ever cheerful, self-contained, and inspiring. They have individuality and are enthusiastically in love with life.

A GOLDFINCH ROMANCE

A GOLDFINCH ROMANCE

ONE late May morning, as I stood in the shadow of a tree by the beaver pond, watching the droll and serious antics of some young beaver, two neatly dressed little birds alighted near and began to eat dandelion seed. They were my first goldfinches. Her call of 'Sweet' was the most bewitching I had ever heard. I lay for a long time among the daisies and watched them. For the first and only time in my life I lost all interest in beaver.

Chattering away merrily like little children, this pair moved quietly about. I followed. Evidently they were young mates. He was handsome with his black cap, olive-green coat, and gold vest almost the color of the dandelion bloom against which he stood. She wore a gray-green gown, with a wash of gold upon her breast.

They seemed so trustful of this good old world, so merry, and so glad to be alive, as they flitted happily among the yellow flowers, I wished that every one might know them. 'Hear me, hear me, dearie,' they called as they fed among the weeds or on the birch buds.

The meal finished, they launched into the air, and to the tune of a cheery 'Per-chic-o-ree, per-chic-o-ree' went swinging through space in long, bounding undulations. They flew in a spirited gallop, as if coasting at high speed over a series of invisible little hills and hollows. I watched them until they flew into the grove. As Mr. Goldfinch alighted, I noted that he was marked by a broken feather.

Two weeks later I saw the pair again, as merry as ever. But why was this young couple not busy nest-building? They probably had been courting for at least six weeks when I first saw them, and they were still at it. I wished that I might have seen the beginning of this long courtship.

It was mid-June, and the robins and the blue-birds by my cabin were working about sixteen hours a day trying to deliver food to nests of youngsters ever shouting for more and more. The chickadees were the only other birds that had not as yet commenced nest-building; usually they selected hollow trees, often abandoned woodpecker or flicker nests of the year before. If they have good reasons for late nesting, I have not discovered them. It is possible that the chickadees that lived around my cabin in winter went farther north, or farther up the mountain to nest; but at any rate there were chickadees in the region practically the year round.

On the Fourth of July I saw the goldfinches again — still courting. He was parading proudly before her, and she proudly watching him. His manner was most winsome. As they galloped away through the air I heard them calling, 'Sweet-eet, sweet-eet,' to each other. These slender little yellow-breasted birds were graceful and charming. Everything they did was appealing.

Never have I seen any bird or being more bewitchingly or inspiringly happy. Often I heard his love song. He sang with ecstasy and in such plaintive, winsome tones as to be intensely thrilling. It was enchanting, enticing, and rapturous. Low and sweetly he talked, long and lovingly he chatted with his mate. Every day, rain or shine, these loving mates went flying about, constantly calling 'Sweet-eet' in their bounding flight through the air. And thus in rapture their courtship went on.

On the 15th of July this vivacious young couple commenced house-hunting. The following day they were building in an alder near the beaver pond. A number of birds and their young children were already starting on the southward migratory journey. Others were bringing their second broods off the nest.

Four days later, when I went back to the alder, I found that the nest was wrecked and abandoned without having been completed. I could find no clue, no one to blame for the damage. But birds have many enemies; often they suffer ill-deserved misfortune.

But it did not end the goldfinch romance. In an alder about fifty feet away I found little Mrs. Goldfinch busy — oh, ever so busy — with another nest. It was about six feet above the ground. Evidently she was of a trusting nature. Shreds of hemplike bark from last year's fallen weeds were being used. She insisted on doing all the work.

While I watched he brought good nesting-material. It must have been good, for she had used it in the first nest. He wanted to weave this into the new nest, but she would not let him. More strangely, she refused, when he gave it to her, to weave it in herself. But, though she refused his material and his assistance again and again, she did it oh so sweetly; there was no scolding.

Another day the little goldfinch home-maker carried off part of the material from the wrecked nest and used it in the new one. Busily the little lady worked. Occasionally she paused to call sweetly to her young and handsome husband, while he, always responsive, was the most gentle and devoted creature that I have seen. Most of the time he sat on a tree-top near by and observed every detail, now and then giving a low call. She as sweetly answered, but without looking up from her nest-building.

If he could not help in the nest-building, at least he was ever on guard for enemies. If very many minutes elapsed after she disappeared for more material, he ceased his song and peered down to catch a glimpse of her. If still she did not return, he gave up doing anything, restlessly looking this way and that, as though thinking, 'I wonder if anything has happened!' With what eagerness and excitement he rushed out to meet her when she came in sight!

Once when I stood close, watching her work, she had been too busy to call or look up for some time. He, with his eye on something in the distance, had neither spoken nor dropped down to see her. Questioningly she called. He was at her side in an instant. 'Sweet,' she answered in all confidence and went on with her work. She did not want a thing, but had to assure herself that her sweet-voiced husband was still around.

I do not know if he extended the luncheon invitation or if she did. But she would suddenly break away from her nest-building, in which she had appeared all concentration, and alight within a few inches of him. After chattering deliciously for a moment, they would go romping off together.

Lovingly the nest was prepared. Built of stringy bark, of fallen plants and grass, it was luxuriously, thickly lined with thistle-down. Quantities of thistle-down were used during the last two days. The little nest-builder had hardly looked up. She was felting and quilting it after her own individual pattern.

The nest completed, Mrs. Goldfinch started to fly off, but turned back and smoothed the lining again. Seating herself in it, she tried the nest, turning first one way and then the other. I doubt if the eggs of any bird in the world rest upon softer or more luxurious beds than those of the goldfinches. Later there were five pale bluish-white eggs.

The Arkansas goldfinch, with yellow dress and heart of gold is one of the treasures of the earth. Wild canary, thistle-bird, yellowbird, and dandelion bird, are some of the names applied to him. His relatives are scattered over the United States and in some localities there is a numerous population. The bird was named from its first discovery on the Arkansas River in Colorado. Like the bluebirds, robins, red-winged blackbirds, Audubon and Townsend warblers, flickers, Audubon hermit thrushes, wrens, and northern violet-green swallows, the Arkansas goldfinches come to the mountain zone to nest and spend the summer. They are always a rare delight. Their gentle ways and sweet disposition would be never-failing antidotes for discontent.

None of the goldfinch family nest early; in fact, they often are the last nest-builders of the season. The males regain their bright color in April, but they are evidently believers in prolonged courtships, and although the nuptial dress is acquired so early, housekeeping is apparently not thought of until July. During three years that I watched them around me, I found that they built between July first and twenty-first.

Most birds time the hatching of their young so that there is an abundant close-to-home food-supply for the youngsters, many of whom daily eat their weight of food. There may be other factors in determining the nesting-time.

Goldfinches eat the seeds of the dandelion, thistle, and sunflower chiefly, where these are obtainable. If you would attract goldfinches (and you would be well repaid for doing so) devote a corner of your garden to sunflowers. Goldfinches perhaps nest late to have a supply of new soft thistle and milkweed down for thickly and softly lining the nest. Or, it may simply be one of their many interesting characteristics.

Mrs. Goldfinch completed the nest on the tenth day; this was quick work, but the material from the wrecked nest may have helped speed up its completion. But even though she speeded up, there was certainly no slighting the job.

I spent much time near the goldfinch nest and discovered other nesting birds. While they had been building, a pair of white-crowned sparrows had brought off a second brood from the willow-clump. Usually for the second nest they go two thousand feet up the mountain-side, where sum-

AN ASPEN WILD-FLOWER GARDEN

mer has just arrived and where food is as abundant as down the mountain a month earlier. I had watched a pair of noisy magpies train their awkward children in the ways considered good in magpie world. Their nest had been a big brush-heap up near the top of an old pine.

The goldfinch alder was one of a clump that stood in an aspen wild-flower garden. Among the aspen were orchids, the silver and blue columbine, tiger lilies with 'heart of fire,' and in late summer the blue fringed gentians. There was always something of interest. I often wished for two or three pairs of eyes. I could have used them.

After my second close approach the goldfinches paid little attention to me, even when I stood near their tree. Nor did they seem to mind other birds alighting near by. They were too absorbed with their own affairs, and with each other. Often the long-crested jays simply shouted from the near-by tree-tops, but this made no difference to the gold-finches.

She sat on the nest nearly all the time; often he brought her something to eat. Sometimes she gave a strangely appealing call. With haste her husband came singing to her side or talked to her in tender, solicitous tone from a near-by limb.

One day, when I appeared from an unusual direction, she gave a startled note of alarm. He darted over to me and then to her. Evidently, judging from his tones, he assured her that I was not in the least dangerous. Having satisfied her, he flew away. But he was constantly near, ever lived for her. And sometimes, without her calling, he went to her — simply, I suppose, because he could not stay away longer.

While Mrs. Goldfinch was off the nest one day, I went up close for a look at the eggs. She returned sooner than expected and alighted on a limb so near that I could have touched her. Looking at me intently, she said, 'Sweet-eet,' as though to ask, 'Aren't they the dearest things in all the world?' Afterwards, she caught me handling the eggs, but did not in any way object and apparently was pleased.

Before the nest was completed the birds often went bathing together in a shallow, sandy little bay of the brook within an easy stone's throw of the nest. Daintily they waded about, occasionally flapping their wings and fluttering in the water. One day a pair of water-ouzels, whose nest was by the brook quite near, stood solemnly, interestedly watching the bathers, who may have appeared to the swimming, diving ouzels as if afraid of the water.

The goldfinch eggs hatched out in fourteen days. Just as I arrived at the nest one day, Mr. Goldfinch came swinging and singing through the air with his bill full of insects for his mate on the nest. He was so happy that he must sing even with his mouth full. One tiny young bird came through the shell that afternoon; I could not tell whether he broke out or whether it was his mother who broke in. She kept leaning over and billing around in the nest, but, fearing to disturb her, I kept back. Two days later, when I returned to the nest, there were five babies, none of them larger than a bumblebee.

The next time I called both old birds were feeding the hungry babies. During the one hundred and twenty-six minutes that I watched, the parents arrived with forty-two loads of supplies. The baby food consisted mostly of plant-lice off nearby grass and leaves, together with a few grubs and beetles.

The five little bits of animated life were interested only in eating, and their parents' only concern was in keeping them fed up. The father seemed much excited over the process. After dropping his holding into a large mouth, he paused to watch the babies, following their every movement eagerly, and looking into each large mouth that continually kept opening. The tiny gaping youngsters were his treasures, and he was in raptures when he left the nest. As he flew away he chirped and warbled, 'Ba-bee, ba-bee,' with utmost love and tenderness.

Seldom did anything come near that might have disturbed the goldfinches. In common with numerous other species of birds, however, they were ready to defend themselves and their young against any odds if necessary. But unlike the robin and some others, they did not worry.

One day, when on a hill-slope east of them, I watched a coyote pass the nesting-tree. Mr. Goldfinch was on top of his favorite dead tree, a fire-killed pine about sixty feet from the nest. Focusing my glasses on him, I wondered what he would do in case the coyote approached too close. He leaned forward and peered down at the coyote, who walked past the nest without a stop. But had he stopped, I believe the little yellow-breasted fellow was ready to hurl himself down at this formidable enemy.

A few days later a wildcat came out of the grove behind the nest. An upstanding limb on a fallen log would enable the cat readily to reach the nest if he tried. Out along this log he walked, when suddenly, 'Spit-t-t-!' He struck right and left at Mr. Goldfinch, then at Mrs. Goldfinch, who came in haste to help her husband.

Of course a robin spread the alarm with wild shouts and rushed to assail the cat. The cries of the robin brought other robins and various birds besides, rushing to the scene to fight off a common invading enemy. The cat backed up against the base of a pine and fought off the birds for some minutes; occasionally he leaped up and forward, striking right and left with fore paws. Twice a robin struck him dangerously near an eye, and he suddenly broke away and ran back into the grove.

These goldfinches raised only one brood of youngsters during the summer. Most other birds around my homestead raised two nestfuls. The

English sparrow and a few other species raise three families each summer.

The youngsters left the nest one afternoon when I could not be there to see this always interesting start into the world. All remained near the nesting-place for a month. I tried to watch for any unusual actions which would indicate that they were leaving for the winter. Most goldfinches of this locality probably winter in Arizona, Texas, and New Mexico.

During much of the year goldfinches go about in small flocks, calling sweetly, chattering pleasantly, and enjoying one another's company. To see a flock of goldfinches feeding on a cold, snowy day is enough to warm any one's heart. No matter how scanty the fare, they eat as leisurely and as goodnaturedly as though amid June's feasts and flowers. They never struggle or contend, but converse in tones sweet and low, often saying, 'Hear me, hear me, dearie.' They are ever so gentle and refined that to be even the uninvited and unnoticed guest at this dinner is a blessing.

You may have been the guest of honor at a grand banquet, where the horn of plenty overflowed, where there was a feast of reason and a flow of soul; but if you want to have a divine touch of Nature, go as an uninvited guest to a goldfinch banquet on some winter day, where all is gentle and genuine, all artistic and inspiring. As you see the dear little birds so happy, you will feel kinder than ever before, and you will live more peacefully and nobly through all life's changing years.

In my observation of birds that commonly live in flocks, they are only equaled in refined and gentle manners by the waxwings. I have never seen them quarreling, but have more than once been fascinated by their cheerfulness, their devotion, and their dainty ways. When feeding they are ever watchful against possible dangers, to which their bright coloring perhaps subjects them to a greater degree than some other birds. But they usually seem successful in fleeing from sneaking cats and swooping hawks.

I was watching by a beaver pond one day, when the goldfinch family, seven strong, alighted near by. The father appeared to have shed some of his gold and black, so that now the dress of all the family was much the same color. The little mother sat for a time on top of a willow watching her family; the children were following the little father about, teasing him to feed them.

As I left the pond (and it was the last time I saw the family) the little father was hanging to a thistle, almost upside down, tearing the seeds apart and scattering them down to the children. The mother sat, like a little statue, on top of a low bush, looking happily on.

Other southbound goldfinches from farther north had been going by for several days. I think my family left early in October, for I did not see them or any other goldfinches after this time. Evidently, unlike most migrants, they travel in the daytime, food-hunting as they go. Although filled with dangers and uncertainties, this migration between summer nesting-home and winter pleasure-resort, is a journey which must be filled with joyous adventures.

During autumn and winter rambles I often peeped into supposedly deserted nests. But usually a big mouse or something else was in possession. It was different with woodpecker holes; I could be sure of finding these in use, especially at night. They are the favorite winter homes of chickadees; and the little 'busy' chipmunk not infrequently hibernates in them. A kingfisher's tunnel nest up the brook from the goldfinch alder was occasionally used by mice and rabbits.

After an autumn shower I passed the goldfinch nest and looked into a little drinking-cup, closely woven like an Indian basket, level full of water. A few days later, as I passed, a little mouse with both fore feet on the rim of the nest was looking down at me. On an October day there were five yellow leaves that recalled to me the Indian legend I had heard regarding the autumn leaves and birds. My winter rambles often took me past the nest, and so I had occasion repeatedly to recall my sweet-voiced goldfinch neighbors. One mild winter day, just after a snowstorm, I glanced to see if the nest still kept its place. It was a brown-frosted little basket heaped with fluffy snow-flakes.

THE WIT-CRACKER JAY

THE WIT-CRACKER JAY

WITH much ado a flock of long-crested jays divided the contents of a vanity-bag which they found by the trail. Each bird that secured a trinket flew with it into a tree for closer examination. One of the jays, carrying a tiny red box in his claw, alighted on a limb near where I was watching. He was followed by three or four other jays, each curious for closer inspection of the article. Handsome fellows they were, in rich dark blue with long tails and high shiny black crests.

The jay with the box eyed it briefly, then began pecking and hammering away at the cover. The cover dropped, and the jay raised the prize in a claw for closer examination. It was a looking-glass and flashed the sunlight in the face of a staring jay close by. With a squawk the bystander back-somersaulted and fled. The other jay spectators also took to the woods.

It fell to my lot to raise an orphan jay, and a most wide-awake youngster he proved. In common with the rest of his species, he had wit — superior mentality — and a definite programme

75

of enjoying himself by shouting, by playing pranks, and by plaguing other fellows in feathers. Only once in a long series of deviltry did I know of his coming to grief — and this from a hen.

A Plymouth Rock with ancient instincts and strong wings flew over the high fence of the hen-yard and hid a nest among bushes. Not knowing the superstition that hens' eggs are not supposed to hatch in high altitudes, she hatched her setting. Full of common sense, too, she used the henyard for food and safety. Nightly she flew over the top and gathered her chicks inside the yard. Each morning after breakfast she flew out and made journeys with her chicks.

One day immediately after a summer shower she and her chicks were spied by the handsome young jay dandy. He flew to the top of a near-by pine, where for some minutes he chuckled — enjoyed in advance the panic he planned to produce. I watched him, little dreaming what was coming — nor did he.

He dived from the tree-top straight for the chicken family. With whistling wings and screech he mimicked a hawk and struck among the scampering chicks beside the startled hen. She kicked

A LONG-CRESTED JAY

LONG-CRESTED JAYS AT FEEDING-TABLE

him flat on his back in the mud, whacked him with
her wings, and trampled him with muddy feet.
He escaped to the tree-top, where he spent an
hour or longer talking to himself while doing
dry-cleaning.

A few weeks later I was writing in the sunshine
just outside my cabin door, when he came along
and eyed me curiously. There was something on
his mind. He was content to shout at a passing
magpie instead of giving the usual chase. Above
my head he clutched the eaves with claws; leaning
far out, head downward and tail in the air, he
gazed at my pencils, then gave a shrill whistle.

As he alighted in the grass near my seat, I
tossed a teddybear toward him. He must have
leaped ten feet into the air. From a near-by tree
he scolded until I put this monster out of sight.
Then he swooped down upon and snatched wildly
at the several pencils, making a caricature of the
pictured emblematic eagle clutching arrows. With
three pencils in his claws he flew to the roof. In
alighting one was knocked from his claws; in trying
to rescue this he dropped another, and both rolled
off the roof. But he clung to the red pencil. The
one that had caught his eye was a large one with

red lead and the maker's name stamped in gilt. Holding this pencil in one claw, he tilted his head and focused one eye upon it as though trying to read the maker's name. He moved it forward and backward as though needing glasses. Finally he bit off part of the red point. After holding it a few seconds he dropped the red point and watched it roll off the roof.

Taking the end of the pencil in one claw and clinging desperately to it, he flew to a near-by tree as though to make his mark. The pencil collided with a twig and was knocked from his grasp. He darted to catch it. In falling it struck a limb and bounded at him. He dodged with a screech. Then he grabbed it in his bill and flew again to the roof. I tossed another pencil near; he scolded and stamped his feet. Carrying the pencil in his mouth with the red point forward, he flew off down the yard.

Why did the name jay ever become synonymous with greenhorn, country bumpkin, and the victim of sharpers? All members of the jay family are famed for their wit. The jay — often a plunderer — is the intellectual of the bird world, and is aristocratic, autocratic, and domineering — the acknowledged superior of other birds. He is handsome, a wearer of bright clothes, and acts and looks the part that should go with royal purple. The European jay runs to the reddish; the American or Eastern jay is light blue; a fellow down by the Rio Grande wears green; while the cock of the family — the wit of wings — the long-crested jay, is clad in deep blue with jet black crest and head and touches of turquoise, purple, and black on wings and tail. The long-crested jay has traits in common with the Eastern blue jay and is about the same size. But he is of superior mentality, a greater personality. He is far more showy, handsome, and aggressive.

The long-crested, or Steller, jay inhabits all the mountain-ranges of western North America and is one of the lords of the earth. He is a character second to none in the entire bird world. He is brilliant, wise, and versatile; he is eternally, efficiently vigilant. If new food comes to his locality, he takes possession before other birds discover it; if new danger arises, he will be the first to detect it; if opportunity for fun is seen, he first uses it; but if there is nothing doing, he starts something.

At one new camp in the woods I had an excess

of food which a home-bound hunter had left for disposal. The jays were cautious as usual, but they quickly discovered that I was harmless. Inside of twenty-four hours every jay within five miles was among those present. For a few days they swarmed over camp. But late one night a young fellow with a gun came along. Not a jay called, and we did not see one near, while he remained. Yet there were loud calls when he showed signs of leaving, and less than five minutes after he left the jays possessed camp.

Generally each spring the numerous jays near my cabin, at nine thousand feet elevation, go up the mountain to timber-line or into the north. But one spring the parents of my young jay evidently concluded to remain and nest where they would have peanuts and raisins rather than the jolly adventures of migration. The nest, built the first week in May, had five eggs. But three youngsters and the two old birds vanished without a clew as to where they had gone.

The second summer my lively jay mated and built a nest in a pine near where his parents had nested. As soon as the nest-building began this noisy fellow became silent. For weeks he had the secret of the nest to keep, and he suppressed his enthusiasm and kept it perfectly. No movement or note of his gave a hint of its location. I discovered it by accident. It was about twenty-five feet up in the pine, and in this six eggs were laid. These hatched, and five youngsters were raised.

Devotedly he carried food to his mate on the nest. To her he was ever most polite and gallant. Often he sat close to her and spoke in low, sweet tones and he sometimes addressed her in a loving, plaintive prattle. The instant the young first called he rushed over the neighborhood making announcements and proclaiming their presence from the tree-tops. Of course he was eager to kick any intruder off the premises and would have protected his family with his life.

The male and the female of this species are identical in dress and disposition. Once the youngsters had left the nest, mother, father, brothers, and sisters all looked so much alike that I could not tell one from the other. The marked difference in appearance of the male and the female of most species of birds — whatever the benefit to them — certainly is a useful arrangement to those who are interested in knowing whether it is he or she. I cannot think of any other species in which the male and female birds are so nearly alike as in the long-crested jay.

These jays feed on the seeds of pines and spruces, they successfully hunt grasshoppers, pick up stray mice, and eat any kind of dead meat found in the wilds. Near camp and cabin they have relished raisins, nuts, candy, corn, wheat, oats, and wild-flower seeds.

As with all red-blooded beings, this jay's bump of curiosity is large, and he must satisfy it. A strange old jay had seen my youngster go into the cabin and come out with wonder raisins. Why not he? Using all his caution, he came to the porch. He alighted in the doorway. He heard something which caused him to back-somersault and retreat with a dash. But he came back and advanced across the floor tiptoe, edging sidewise, with eyes and ears working, ready to escape quickly. And thus a jay often explores, dares possible dangers, but is wary of possible ambush.

He is a scout. Never does his curiosity or eagerness betray him into danger. Seeing something at a distance that he simply must know about, he will dart around, squawk, circle, and do all he can to draw out possible danger. It must be safe and sane before he advances for a close look at the new object.

Often he is a soldier of fortune; his love of adventure is predominant. His is adventure for the fun of it; he is without concern as to whether this troubles or amuses those who have second parts thrust upon them by himself. With endless energy and alertness, his incessant stir must be an evolutionary factor in the bird world, stimulating wide-awakeness.

It appears a part of the daily program of a crested jay to amuse himself by causing disturbance among neighboring birds. A flock of goldfinches were cheerily feeding among the wild flowers of my yard, when a jay from the closest tree hurled himself among them like a hawk. They retreated in a panic. Yet they were not feeding on anything that he wanted. He flew back into the tree-top and jeered in glee.

Another time a jay disturbed a flock of pine siskins that were feeding in tree-tops on aspen catkins. Often I have seen him drive chipmunks into hiding, and it is common for him to dash unannounced upon a robin, evidently just to heckle.

In fact, he enjoys a daily row with robins. They often meet for a few hot words. A deadly war ever seems impending, but rarely are blows exchanged.

Robins and jays often nest in the same neighborhood. Both are good policemen and scouts, and rarely does a hawk venture into the region. And woe to the owl that concludes to have a quiet day in the territory enjoyed by robins and jays! He is almost certain to be discovered and his whereabouts and undesirable presence noised over the neighborhood.

Though useful to other birds in fighting off birds of prey, the jay is not popular. Ever crafty and quarrelsome, he is too much given to scolding, persecuting, and even stealing from other birds. He is accused of sometimes robbing nests of their eggs and even of their young. Perhaps a jay sometimes does, but this I think is rare, it is not a general custom of the species. At least, I have never seen him take eggs or young from a nest.

The jay is eager to talk, freely gives opinions and advice. He has a keen interest in world affairs, and his mind is quickly made up. Of course, having opinions and decisions, he is eager to express himself publicly.

He is also eager to show other accomplishments. Like all great talkers, he wants a big audience, and sometimes secures a mixed one by raising his crest and hollering. This alarm call brings all bird neighbors pell-mell to the scene. His vocabulary is unequaled, and his utterances express love, victory, war, distress, and anguish; his tones are appealing, mandatory, insinuating, oratorical, and wise.

But rarely does he show a sense of values. He may declare war on a grasshopper or a hawk with equal energy. A peculiar cry brings every bird in the neighborhood, ready to follow his leadership and repel a monstrous invader. But this cry may be uttered when there is nothing to repel. If there is a big job, he handles it alone and boasts of it afterward. He is ever hollering and parading round; constantly raising and lowering and gesturing with his crest. With expressive crest and attitude he displays curiosity, anger, contempt, pride, and superiority. Yet these noisy birds take life seriously and during nesting-time are retiring and silent.

Much of the time this jay is with a flock of his

own species; sometimes with mixed flocks of magpies and Clark nutcrackers. Full of energy and ability, he likes to entertain all birds with speech or prank or be among those present when some other fellow is entertaining. In amazement I have watched crowds of jays do their stunts. There was endless mockery.

Though a rare personality himself, the long-crested jay takes ideas from the birds round him. Often he applies the idea more efficiently than the specialist from whom it was appropriated. He excels in the climbing and acrobatic stunts of woodpeckers, crossbills, and chickadees. The climbing performances of slow parrots he does on high gear.

One day I saw a matter-of-fact and good-natured woodpecker stop and admire a jay peck open a nut. When cracking something the jay stands on a limb or other secure spot with the object clutched between his toes. Tilting back, he swings body, neck, and head forward, his bill striking the object like a pick. He hits rapidly and with surprising force.

In carrying off shelled peanuts to the young or to store for times of food-shortage, he takes from four to seven nuts in his mouth, then one in his bill, and, bursting with treasures, flies leisurely away. The food is placed under bark or in cracks of a dead tree. But if there is much to be stored, the objects are placed in the thick needle-clusters or in the heart of weed-clumps.

One day a few friends oversupplied my jay with shelled and non-shelled peanuts, together with raisins, bits of chocolate, and sandwiches. The richness of opportunity excited him, and he hurried to store all that he could among the needles of a near-by pine. The first few he concealed, but after this he aimed simply to place the nuts or raisins where they would stay, though they were in plain sight. After loading the pine with the fullness of a Christmas-tree he flew off.

An hour later, when the jay came shouting back to the cabin, a gray Frémont squirrel was busy harvesting his Christmas-tree. He darted like lightning and knocked the surprised squirrel off a limb, then pursued and battered him all over the tree, with wings and bill, until the squirrel found a place of safety behind thick small limbs. The squirrel from this refuge gave the jay a large-sized piece of his mind.

This jay had keen eye-sight and good memory — the common qualities of his tribe. Often I threw nuts or raisins into the grass while he was not apparently looking, and even when I knew he was watching something else. But down he would drop and without hesitation pick up the prize.

I tossed four peanuts in rapid succession into the grass — to the right, to the left, to the right, and then at the jay. He watched from a tree limb about ten feet from me. The nuts fell about four feet apart, and as the last one bounced, he flew toward it and picked it out of the tall grass. Then he flew to each of the others, not in the order in which they fell, but to the one nearest him. He went directly to each nut, something I could not have done. Another of his species was tried out, and readily duplicated the same performance.

Even when tamed and subdued, the jay maintains a certain wildness, an inquiring interest in the new, and an individuality that never surrenders to ease or routine. My jay wanted to examine every new thing, and he had more than a superficial interest in it. Sometimes he would become impatient and stamp his feet if not successful in fathoming the mystery quickly.

A glass twine-holder on the table caused him long entertainment. He walked round it, pecked it, and tried to peep in where the string came out. I held it up for him to view and pulled out several yards of string. While still examining it he became entangled in the loose string. He darted out of the cabin, with a squawk, pulling the string with him. Unable to untangle it, he alighted and fought it. He was not panic-stricken nor afraid. He leaped into the air and came down stiff-legged upon the string, beating it with his wings.

I have never seen the equal of this jay as a mimic. The mockingbird is an adept at reproducing the songs of other birds — and so is this fellow. But he mimics songs, calls, squawks, warnings, threats, and actions with marked success and often to the astonishment or confusion of the birds mimicked. In California I heard one confidently and successfully imitating a mockingbird.

The first time that my jay youngster saw a flock of crossbills he gave full attention to their climbing through the tops of bushes and among the outer twigs of pines, getting easily into every possible position. I imagined that later he would try to repeat their performances, and perhaps he did. But he immediately mimicked the bell-like notes and strange calls that the crossbills give continuously while feeding.

His species is known for harsh squawks and calls. Yet he is a singer. He is exceedingly alert and shy and keeps well away from people, and many who have known the jay for years never dreamed of his ability as a singer. Yet he sometimes sings an hour at a stretch, one song after another; it may be his own or it may be a reproduction of another bird. Many times I have watched the jay plainly rehearsing — trying over and over again to perfect a mimicked song or call. This practice is performed with contentment and immense satisfaction.

The jay is progressive. Though he spends most of his time with the noisy crowd having a rollicking time, he does enjoy being alone and frequently deliberately withdraws from the crowd. In the privacy of a leafy tree-top he sits and thinks; he philosophizes, he talks to himself, he holds a whispered conversation with an imaginary bird; he rehearses, calls, and sings, and perhaps he plans some new pestiferous surprise on feathered neighbors.

He is full of surprises, and there ever is something doing when he is around. He is watchful for new advantages, and is the first to try new fields.

The long-crested, or Steller, jay is the most talked-about fellow in his territory. He is ever in the public eye. The hawk is an unseen bogy to many birds, but every bird knows of the noisy and prank-loving jay, and numbers have a speaking acquaintance with him.

He ranges over Western America wherever there are forests and is seen at the seashore and up through the mountains, and he even explores above the timber-line. His voice and colors have welcomed me in nearly every far-off wilderness visited. In Mexico, California, and Vancouver and on the summit of Long's Peak in the Rockies, he has been the wit and clown of my lonely rambles. Once in the mountains of Colorado I came upon him in magnificent pose standing upon the back of a grand old grizzly that stood in repose. Here, together, were the two dominating wilderness characters that most impressed me among a thousand camp-fires.

THE PTARMIGAN AT HOME

THE PTARMIGAN AT HOME

THE high-lying mountain plateaus are lands strangely full of life and romance. These magnificent distances up in the sky are a novel scene. Nowhere is there a solitary pine to check or tune the wild and heedless winds; it is a ragged-edged realm with numerous out-reaching plateaus and mesas, without the sheltering, softening influence of grove or forest.

Walking among the stunted, half-buried trees at timber-line one snowy, bright winter day, I narrowly escaped stepping upon a snow-white ptarmigan that had been squatting in its little hollowed-out depression in the snow. It ran a short distance, then, squatting, became invisible. I startled a second ptarmigan, then a third, before realizing it must be a flock. Ten or fifteen rose at once with a loud cackle and flew high over the snow to an outjutting ridge. Their dazzling white bodies were impressively beautiful against the clear, bright-blue winter sky.

Except in the nesting-season, ptarmigan are most often seen in flocks. The ptarmigan, sometimes called 'mountain quail,' and the leucosticte, or rosy finch, are the highest-ranging and most alpine of all birds in Colorado. Occasionally, during prolonged storms, they may descend below timber-line even two or three thousand feet, but they are permanent residents of the heights. In these lower scenes they appear to have a rollicking vacation.

I once planned to get close to a flock of ptarmigan by going on all fours. They were in their summer garb and barely discernible as they moved quietly about their feeding-ground. When within perhaps fifteen feet of them I stopped. They were coming towards me. Occasionally one snapped at a fly, ate a leaf, or grabbed a grasshopper. There were twenty-five or more in the flock. Presently all were around me. Three or four went beneath me, several passed close in front, and two in pursuit of something ran between my arms. They must have considered me a rock, if they even considered me. To them perhaps I was simply part of the topography.

They moved on so slowly that I finally became tired of being a quadruped. Glancing up, I saw two mountain sheep watching me closely from a

THE SUMMER AND WINTER HOMES OF THE PTARMIGAN AND
THE ROSY FINCH ABOVE TIMBER-LINE

near-by boulder-pile. Evidently they could not classify me. The muscles of my neck and back ached, but I tried to hold my place until the ptarmigan were well out of the way. At last I allowed myself to slowly settle to the grass, where I stretched out at full length. I could not see where the sheep stood without moving; but I could hear the low clucking or conversation which the ptarmigan continually carried on.

Soon this conversation became more distinct. Evidently the entire flock was returning. While waiting I watched a high-soaring eagle. He must have been three thousand feet above me, and where I lay the altitude was nearly thirteen thousand feet. As he circled lower, his shadow rushed across near-by rocks where a marmot, sunning himself, gave a clear, scolding whistle and fled.

In summer the marmot population above timber-line is a numerous one. His shrill whistle, like a traffic policeman's, penetrates the unobstructed distances with an inquiring 'Who goes there?' But he seldom waits for an answer. Before you approach he scrambles awkwardly off his boulder and disappears into his den. He is of a darker color than his lowland cousin, the woodchuck or ground hog, but has the same habits of taking long sun-baths throughout the summer and hibernating dur-ing winter. One marmot at Keyhole on the Long's Peak trail has shared many a lunch with climbers who tarried at this point to await the return of their party from the ascent to the top. Food and patience, sitting quietly, will bring almost any wild thing into our acquaintance.

I had flattened myself out on the ground wait-ing for the flock of ptarmigan. Something must have frightened them. They came running past my feet and head. Two leaped upon me, followed by others. One jumped off on the opposite side, but the rest stood for a few seconds, looking about, not considering me at all. Then all but one stepped off and went slowly forward. The last one walked along my side and for a moment used my shoulder for a viewpoint. Then he came stamp-ing over my head and cheek before leaping down into the low-growing grass. Then he turned for a look at me as though it had just occurred to him that I might be something alive. Being unable to decide, he turned and went leisurely on, considering only his own affairs. When I rose, the ptarmigan were out of sight. The word 'ptarmigan' is probably from the Gaelic 'tarmachan,' meaning 'mountaineer.' The ptarmigan is found on the highest wind-swept hills of the British Isles, on the snowy summits of the Rocky Mountains as far south as the Taos range in northern New Mexico, around the Arctic Circle, on the long chain of the Aleutian Islands, and across the Arctic tundras of North America from Labrador to western Alaska.

In Colorado it breeds from eleven thousand feet to the summit of many high peaks and winters at timber-line. It feeds on the buds of dwarfed willows in winter. In summer it adds grasshoppers, caterpillars, beetles, and other insects which the alpine plants support to its diet of leaves, grasses, and flowers.

The ptarmigan nests above timber-line among the jagged rocks and boulders, the nest being merely a depression on the ground, lined with a little grass or leaves or a few feathers. Finding such a nest is almost pure accident, for if the ptarmigan has attained the utmost protection for itself in its concealing plumage and slow movements, it has gone still further in concealing its nest.

I was watching two ptarmigan, wondering if they had a nest somewhere near. In the midst of the watching a mountain sheep and her two little lambs appeared on a ridge near by. I turned to watch them for perhaps half a minute. A cliff of rocks rose behind the ptarmigan, and a ridge of boulders barred one side of them. As I stood in the open before them, I felt that even while watching the sheep the ptarmigan could not get away without my knowing it.

But when I turned to look for them, they were nowhere to be seen. I was certain that they had not flown away. I advanced to the spot where I had last seen one of them and stood looking all around. Then I made a series of concentric circles, examining the ground closely. Not locating either of the birds, I returned to the spot where one had been. I had about decided to give up the search, when one of them commenced to peck my shoe. I was standing so close that I was actually touching her with my toe.

On another occasion a ptarmigan rose for a short distance and lighted. I walked to the spot and searched and searched without finding it. I sat down on a boulder, looked about, wrote notes, and looked about some more. In the midst of this waiting a gust of wind blew my hat off. In grab-

THE PTARMIGAN IN AUTUMN PLUMAGE

THE PTARMIGAN AT TWELVE THOUSAND FEET

bing for the hat I nearly struck the ptarmigan, which was sitting patiently on a near-by boulder, waiting for me to leave first.

Remarkable changes of plumage take place twice a year, this semiannual moult providing the bird with perfect concealment from its enemies at any season. In winter, when its range is mostly snow-covered, it is robed in pure white, even to its feathered legs and feet. Its bill and eyes are shining black. At other seasons its mottled brown and gray and white plumage blends so perfectly with the gray-brown granite rocks and scattered patches of dirty snow that it is almost impossible to locate.

The ptarmigan has mastered the fine art of living in regions seemingly uninhabitable. But even with its perfect adaptation of dress, it has much to contend with from the fox, bear, lion, and weasel. The weasel, or ermine, has its own white winter suit, which serves as an advantage to it in securing its prey in the same degree that the ptarmigan's white dress is beneficial. Around mining camps the ptarmigan has been considerably reduced in numbers, because of its edibility, and because of its utter lack of fear making it comparatively easy to catch.

In wandering the bleak, snowy heights in winter I came to love this rare bird. Often as I passed near a flock on snowshoes, they would watch me silently but at the same time with confidence and seeming satisfaction. They are the silent birds of the silent peaks. Their few, brief calls are hoarse and strange. They cannot be translated into English words. The notes are generally of inquiry or alarm. On rare occasions a number of these birds will join in a brief, rattling chorus which suggests the efforts of the guinea. The call of the male bird slightly resembles the call of a turkey. The quiet movements and silence of this alpine bird make its presence very impressive to the lonely visitor. I have never met beast or bird that is so expressive in the language of silence. They dearly want to be intimate, but they never say so. The ptarmigan has won my heart wherever I have found it among the crags or on the small willow-dotted tundras. Its deliberateness, its self-containedness, and its bold life among the wild, lonely scenes combined to give me a strong attachment for it.

The ptarmigan enjoys the wild mountain blizzards, and in the headlong whirl of the snow it is as much at home as a duck on the waves. In running it generally goes forward with a series of spurts and pauses, the frequency and duration of these pauses decreasing as the speed is increased. It flies but little, but when its wings are used, its manner of flight is very like that of the prairie chicken.

In June or early July the proud mother ptarmigan leaves her rude nest on the ground and struts about with from six to fifteen lively little cotton balls. The young ptarmigan grow up among some of the most beautiful and healthful scenes on earth. They live on the very roof of the world. The alpine meadows which they ramble are scattered with snowdrifts and strewn with bright flowers.

Donald MacMillan in 'Four Years in the White North' has the following record of ptarmigan: 'Common at Etah in spring and fall migration. Not seen in July and August. Undoubtedly many remain in far North throughout the year. Seen on March 19, 1914, when we were crossing the Beitstadt Glacier of Ellesmere Land at a height of 4,700 feet, with a temperature of 50° F. These birds pick through the crust of snow with their bill, then clear away loose snow with their feet, in order to uncover willow buds. The breeding note in April resembles very much the sound of a policeman's rattle. Nesting date early in June.'

Stefansson in 'The Friendly Arctic' has several references to ptarmigan, the following on Lougheed Island (at the extreme edge of the Arctic Ocean): 'The summer brought but one flock of ptarmigan and the ducks were only king eiders and old squaws. Plovers probably do not go that far north but there were sandpipers, snow buntings, owls, and the same three kinds of gulls noted farther north. It goes without saying that there were no signs of Eskimos.'

Hudson Stuck in 'The Ascent of Denali' (Mount McKinley) makes the following comment: 'At this camp (ten thousand feet) at the head of the glacier we saw ptarmigan on several occasions, and heard their unmistakable cry on several more, and once we felt sure that a covey passed over the ridge above us and descended to the other glacier. It was always in thick weather that these birds were noticed at the glacier head, and we surmised that perhaps they had lost their way in the cloud.

'But even this was not the greatest height at

which bird life was encountered. In the Grand Basin, at sixteen thousand, five hundred feet, Walter was certain that he heard the twittering of small birds familiar throughout the winter in Alaska, and this also was in the mist. I have never known the boy make a mistake in such matters, and it is not essentially improbable. Doctor Workman saw a pair of choughs at twenty-one thousand feet, on Nun Kun in the Himalayas.'

The ptarmigan and the rosy finch together possess these treeless heights of the Rockies the year round. One cold, snowy day I took shelter under a rock cliff and found a flock of rosy finches had found this refuge ahead of me. Quietly, almost gladly, they allowed me to share their shelter from the storm. They nest as high as thirteen thousand feet, upon the rocks.

The treeless area in the San Juan mountains of Colorado is unusually impressive. In it, the sky prairie is well grassed, comparatively level and smooth, and it is one of the highest and possibly the highest, table-land of like area in the world. It reposes at about thirteen thousand feet. It is surrounded by a magnificent near-by wall of rugged peaks and commands splendid views down into the surrounding valleys.

Mountain-tops have comparatively little snowfall. Often during a snowstorm, as well as during a rainstorm, the region above the timber-line is above the storm-line. The region of greatest snowfall is the middle slopes of the mountains; the mountain-tops in most localities have a comparatively dry climate. The yearly weather story of the alpine heights is one of the most interesting in weather lore. Go to the summits for sunshine. The air is clear. Everything is serene. Night after night on the heights stars crowd as nowhere else.

Peaks have their storms, but in all my experience I know of their being struck by lightning only a few times. Often, however, the air of the heights is surcharged with electricity while a storm is below. Wonderful are the terrific winds of the high plateaus. They sometimes boom and roar for hours, beating against the crags and rushing through passes, with a speed of more than one hundred miles an hour. Occasionally, while exploring two miles above the sea, I watched a storm come to the world below. The peak's slopes were encircled and the lowlands covered. Sub-

THE PTARMIGAN AT HOME IN WINTER WITH SNOW AND SUNSHINE

dued thunders rolled and echoed beneath the
clouds; their upper surface — their silvery lining
— broke and rolled around rocky headlands like
the sea, and there were brilliant rainbows in the
scenes below, while high peaks stood thoughtful
in the sunlight.

From the heights one sees the cloud scenes —
clouds large and small — clouds like detached
high mountains and low, wide plains — come and
go. One sees close at hand the under sides of
clouds, their edges, slopes, peaks, cañons, and
summits.

The utter absence of trees in the heights gives
a desert effect and makes it a strange world by
itself. Timber-line in the Rockies is the wavering and far-reaching shore of the vast forest sea
that lies deep and wide over the irregular surface
of the mountains below. And also it is the shore-
line of the treeless, island-like lands that stand
above it. This treeless realm is not a solid mass,
but appears an archipelago in the sky, made up
of many long, large, deeply indented islands, with
small outlying islands in clusters and isolated ones
off by themselves. Stretches are extensive table-
lands, cut with a few short deep cañons and piled

with picturesque buttes. Other areas are occupied by peaks that tower in clusters or extend to the horizon in single file.

These areas above eleven thousand, five hundred feet are a numerously populated life-zone in summer, and have grasslands, fields of wild flowers, and many birds and animals to their highest points. There are places, acres in extent, deeply overlaid with rich soil, and countless spaces and patches of soil at the foot of cliffs, on ledges, in boulder-fields, and between shattered rock-fragments. Wherever soil is found, it is pretty certain in summer to be covered with sedges, grasses, and brilliant wild flowers — flowers of red, yellow, blue, and orange; flowers on tall, slender stalks in the shelter of boulders and rock-crevices; and low-growing dwarfed blossoms that cling to the earth almost stemless.

Many an eternal snow-field has a fringe of colored bloom. Around it bees hum, and here butterflies with intentionally pretty wings add decoration and charm. These varicolored gardens are of as many sizes and forms as the silken cloud shadows that are so strangely, definitely projected against the alpine land.

There are matted growths of arctic willow and dwarfed black birch along the alpine streams. Here many visiting birds nest and sing. Many birds, probably the majority of species, raise two broods each year. They may build a new nest for the second brood. In the Rockies the white-crowned sparrow and the broad-tailed humming-bird nest early among the mid-slope flowers, at nine thousand feet or lower, and then move up the slope two or three thousand feet higher to be among the alpine flowers and insects while the second brood of children grow up. Summer comes later to the heights, and they are able to raise both broods of children in its warmth and in the midst of abundant food-supply. Here the paint-brush is at its reddest — a favorite with mountain hummingbirds.

The mountain nesting-habits of these and other species have often led me to wonder if there may not be lowland birds, who, after hatching one brood, travel several hundred miles farther into the north and raise the second family. In most places a thousand feet of altitude supplies many of the conditions given by a thousand miles of latitude. The complications which these mountains introduce, the numerous varieties of birds found in a small area, and the other features which they maintain, give increased interest to the whole story of bird life and travels.

The temperature and climatic conditions of these heights being somewhat similar to those of the polar world of the Arctic, they appeal to many of the same species of birds and plants. Some species of birds, of the same kind that nest in the Far North, come to this mountain realm from the far southland and use it for their summer nesting-place; while others, who winter in the lowlands of these mountains, make the short migratory flight of an hour or less up the slopes and there, above the timber-line, nest and raise their young. These few birds have a short, easy, migratory journey, but they must miss a most interesting experience. I cannot imagine anything more delightful than the journey most birds have in the long migratory flight from the southland to the Arctic Circle or the mountain heights, and then the return journey when the autumn colors paint the land.

One June I camped at twelve thousand feet, just above the timber-line. Late in the evening I heard the robins and the solitaires singing in the woods below. Near me the ptarmigan and the rosy finches conversed and called to their kind. In a brook before my camp I saw an ouzel, and a pair of white-crowned sparrows hopped about among the dwarfed willows. Other summer bird neighbors of the ptarmigan are the American pipit and the junco.

On a dry moor back of camp I saw a Wilson's warbler, a horned lark, and a Savannah sparrow. One night a long-eared owl flew silently by. Among the birds that evidently were just flying visitors from the woods below, were the alpine three-toed woodpecker, the Western bluebird, one of the fly-catchers, and a number of noisy Clark nut-crackers.

The presence of a woodpecker above the limits of the woods occasioned a mild surprise. But a greater surprise to me was a visit from the camp-robber — the Rocky Mountain gray jay. This species lives in the seclusion of the deep woods and rarely does it venture far into the open. Perhaps he espied my camp; the instinct of this bird to visit the camps of people is simply irresistible. Although they sometimes come for company or to satisfy curiosity, the chief motive is for food.

This visitor eagerly lunched with me. Perhaps he came with this expectation.

Each autumn wild life congregate to feast and frolic in the heights. To this feast come little and big fellows in their furs and many a bird of fine feathers. There are birds and beasts of prey to fatten on the feasters. There are a few thousand birds. Many come a thousand miles or more from the North; others come up the mountain-side a few thousand feet. Many live in the neighborhood, or are cradled in near-by scenes. They are resting, playing, and exploring. But when the colored leaves are falling, the birds young and old go far away to the warm southland. The winds and snows make merry in the scenes where they loved and sang and happily raised their children for their brief, adventurous life. What, I wonder, are the thoughts of the ptarmigan when the sweet, uneasy note of the bluebird tells of southland dreams?

In this strange, alluring mountain-top world I have spent many a week, in winter and in summer, camping along the alpine streams and exploring rocky peaks. Always there was life around me, birds and animals leading their busy, happy lives beyond the front ranks of the forest.

This treeless realm is overspread with a million silvery rootlets of several mighty rivers. Beautiful lakes, with rocky boundaries, are scattered along the farthest edge of the forest. Around these lakes many birds gather, to drink and bathe and to feed. Sit beside any lake or stream and you will have innumerable glimpses of bird-life. Whether they nest near by or afar, birds will come to rest and play, or perhaps — who knows? — just to visit.

CALLING ON BIRDS

CALLING ON BIRDS

OUT on the Great Plains an eagle darted by me straight for an antelope kid. The kid had just got up and was stretching his legs. Perhaps he heard, saw, or scented his approaching mother. In less than an instant the eagle would have struck the kid, but for the mother antelope. With lightning-like flash she leaped between the eagle and its intended victim.

The eagle swerved, circled with angry cries, and darted at another kid, which leaped to its feet, perhaps startled out of its 'freezing' by the eagle's sudden approach. It leaped to safety beneath its mother's sheltering body.

Twice thwarted, when each strike had seemed certain, the eagle simply screeched with anger. But the end was not yet. It circled above the antelope with watchful waiting, determined to have a kid.

Just why an antelope mother seeks seclusion when the kids are born, and why she remains in seclusion, away from the defensive assistance of other antelope mothers, is not understood. But it must be that this custom is, or has been, of advantage to the species.

Wolves and eagles have the antelope at a disadvantage by attacking her when she is alone and with two weak, wobbly-legged children, and none of her kind near to distract or attack the enemy. And her home environment would seem a disadvantage, the wide, treeless plains offer so little concealment and so few hiding-places. Not until the youngsters become fleet-footed does the mother join others.

Alone this mother met the repeated attacks of this powerful and persistent eagle. Unable to strike a kid while darting at high speed, the eagle tried to seize one. It circled, swooped, feinted, trying to frighten the kids out from beneath their mother's protecting body, and beyond the reach of her swiftly striking fore feet.

The eagle then tried fluttering just over the mother antelope, swerving this way and that, feinting and darting at her eyes to force her to dodge, to make an opening. Turning quickly to right and to left, the antelope evaded these thrusts and kept her head and fore feet toward the eagle's advances.

Occasionally she reared up and struck at the eagle with fore feet, or leaped high to do this. Her movements were lightning-like and she used her small sharp-edged hoofs tellingly. One of these strokes broke a quill from the eagle's wing, and only missed breaking the wing by the fraction of an inch. The eagle needed all his skill and speed to avoid these attacks, any one of which if effective would break wing or neck.

The kids stood side by side beneath the mother's body. Flying low and circling quickly, the eagle with sudden darts tried on first one side then the other to seize a kid.

Round and round the mother turned as the eagle circled; now to the right, now to the left, responding to the movements of the attacker. Beneath the mother the two youngsters constantly worked in unison with her movements, constantly used her body as a shield.

Both the eagle and the antelope were tiring; they had sustained a terrific pace for fifteen or twenty minutes. The eagle was displaying almost reckless daring. Neither was striking with his earlier skill.

This lack of skill appeared due more to weary

eyes than to weakened muscles. The eagle still wheeled with swiftness, darted with speed. The antelope still moved with spring and struck with quickness. It appeared probable that their eyes had failed or weakened.

The eagle has long-range, high-power eyes; the antelope, perhaps more than any other big animal, has telescopic eyes, developed perhaps by the needs on wide and treeless plains.

In the midst of this wavering of skill came the unexpected. With one of the mother's quick moves one of the youngsters failed to move in unison. He tripped or stepped into a hole and stumbled. Instantly the eagle wheeled and struck at it. Just as quickly the mother whirled toward it and with quick second move leaped high and struck with fore feet at the eagle.

She landed, but perhaps glancingly, upon the eagle's tilted back. The eagle was knocked to the grass, followed by fluttering, scattered feathers. Again the mother leaped high and came down with four feet together as she would in killing rattlesnakes. But with heavy flutter the eagle moved and she missed. Then with low flight, the wings making effort with every slow stroke, the eagle retreated across the prairie. The mother and kids stood in repose, looking after the eagle.

Then I roused myself. During all this while I had stood near by watching every move, forgetful of all else. I had a camera but forgot it; in fact I was all concentration on this contest. But when it ended, I was gripping my hatchet handle with all my might.

Three pairs of golden eagles nested near my cabin the first two years after I built it. Both during flight and while perched on tree-top or cliff one of the pair showed distinctly larger than the mate. Once I came close while a pair were at rest upon a cliff, and the larger of the two appeared to be about double the weight of the other. I supposed, that, as with other birds, the larger of the two was the male. It was more than a year before I discovered my mistake. The smaller eagle in each of the three pairs I had watched was the male.

I became interested in eagles, for I thought I might discover some other unusual facts. After watching them scores of times soaring by the hour higher than the top of Long's Peak, I concluded that this soaring was their recreation, just a kind of play for eagles. Trying to learn just what the eaglets were fed gave me many interesting days and several exciting bits of cliff-climbing.

I also discovered that it took about four months to raise the two eaglets. A finch will build a nest, lay, hatch, and send forth a family of four in four weeks. The length of incubation did not vary greatly in the other birds I had watched. The goldfinch's eggs hatched in fourteen days, and a red-winged blackbird's eggs had also taken fourteen; a bluebird by my cabin brought young ones through the shells on the twelfth day, while a mother hummingbird hatched her one egg in thirteen days. But I recalled that a bob-white's eggs on a farm in Kansas had taken twenty-four days to hatch, although I had planned to have shells bursting on the fifteenth day.

I found that eagles mated for life and that they usually hunted together. They are a match for any animal of their size and for some larger ones. They ever eat warm blood. It is no wonder that wild life fears them, even sheep with young lambs, which are readily exposed to their long-range vision on the unsheltered heights where they soar.

I had much profitable fun watching the birds

A HIGH PLATEAU IN THE ROCKIES

around my boyhood cabin in the mountains. This was before the days of popular bird-guides. But I had a speaking acquaintance with many birds; that is, I was familiar with their identification marks, knew their nesting and home habits and much about their methods of making a living, long before I knew their scientific names. I believe that being intimately acquainted with even one species, is far more interesting and worth while than merely knowing the names of dozens.

I often wondered concerning the mental processes of birds in the spring. What can be the thoughts and the conversations which occur between resident birds and the bird travelers who come into the locality in the summer. Do the visiting birds bring with them a worldliness, an air of superiority, or do they come filled with stories of adventure and eager to learn more of new scenes? Do the rural birds welcome the newcomers, or do they look upon them with distrust? What do they think of each other, these travelers and the resident birds, when they meet and mingle, as they frequently do, during the days of leisure which commonly precede the birds' nesting?

Bluebirds and red-winged blackbirds from the

south arrived near my cabin about the first week of March. But they played around for a month or six weeks before thinking of the work of home-making. A series of old beaver ponds that had filled in a generation or more before was overgrown with the high grass and a thick network of willow-clumps. Here the blackbirds swung and sang.

I thought I was completely concealed one morning in a wet, grassy flat close to where a young redwing was hidden. His parents, especially the handsome father with a small red decoration on each shiny black wing, set up a great ado and tried to drive me off. He darted at me so viciously, striking with outstretched wings, and demanded my departure so insistently, that I finally moved on.

Circling in search of other youngsters who might be trying to become reliable flying-machines, I discovered that this red-winged father was busy protecting two sets of youngsters. Feathers found in the grass led me to believe that one father might have been killed. It is common for birds to help care for orphans of the same species in case of disaster. But there may not have been a death.

The following spring this handsome black fellow with red and yellow wing decorations had two wives and two nests to defend. I have since found a few other redwings with two families. This may occasionally be the case with other species of birds also. But this was just one of the thousand interesting, unexpected things that a bird-watcher discovers.

This particular scolding redwing boldly followed me for some distance. He certainly said a number of vigorous things, and finally, alighting on a willow within a few feet of me, he hurled something at me that may have been, 'Get out of here, and no more prowling around in this grassy, willowy territory of mine while the youngsters are trying to fly; you have never caused me trouble before, but I do not propose to let you step on the children.' He finally turned back, and I went on to the beaver pond down stream.

The Rocky Mountain gray jay — 'camp-robber' — is the earliest nest-builder that I have seen. He was sitting on eggs in the last week in February. These eggs may not have hatched, but later I saw young camp-robbers in the last week of March. This would mean that the nest must have been ready about the first of March and the eggs laid soon after. These birds are omnivorous eaters, and it is probable that they had a year-round food-supply. Their food consists of meat, nuts, seeds, willow buds, and, when near human habitation, anything available. Apparently they often store food for future consumption.

In most localities hawks and owls are thought to be the first spring egg-layers. I have seen young owls late in March and young hawks early in April, but without seeing the nest-building. Evidently hawks and owls hatch in advance of most other birds in order that their young may be fed, at least in part, upon the eggs and young of later-nesting birds.

The nesting-habits of birds fill one of the most interesting chapters in natural history. Early and late nesting, long and short courtships, the mating songs and calls, and the plumage assumed by some birds at this season give birds an individuality not unlike ourselves. Observing them in their domestic affairs, their devotion to each other, their care and defense of their young, and the training of the children for life raises birds in our estimation and brings them into our sympathies and understanding.

I once watched a pair of robins in their efforts to get a house built. He evidently did not know prevailing etiquette and insisted on helping. She finally made a scene in declining his assistance. He was allowed to bring the mud, but not to do the plastering — he was merely the hod-carrier. The first time he came with a mouthful of grass and the best of intentions she shouted angry 'tuts' and 'phits' at him. He sat and looked sober but held to the grass. He offered it again. She stormed. He went off to eat worms. An hour later he came back and this time with a precious string — one of the treasures which so many robins weave into the structure of the house. She was busy and did not see him until he alighted, all too close to the nest. With much ado she drove him off the premises.

The water-ouzel builds her nest close to the splashing brook, under the very bank or on a rocky ledge. This is a bulky affair, open on the side, constructed of sticks and moss. It is well camouflaged for its location, and is one of the most difficult of nests to locate. Unless you should be looking at the nest at the time its occupants were entering or leaving it, in all probability you would look in vain.

A pair of neighbor ouzels one June built two nests. I never saw them make any use of the second one. Possibly it was for protection. A few species of birds build an extra nest to camouflage the existence of the one used. In case of danger they show themselves by the empty nest. This is similar to the pretext which birds sometimes employ of being crippled, endeavoring to lead the enemy out of the vicinity of the nest, by tumbling and fluttering away from it.

I discovered a warbler with a bit of grass in her bill and watched for the nest-building. Apparently oblivious of my presence, she went on with the work. A few days later I found that she and her mate had almost completed a nest in a tree behind me, and this nest I watched was built to fool me evidently.

Most birds carry all chips, straws, and refuse some distance from the nest, so as not to advertise its presence. The woodpecker or other bird that fails to do this is likely to betray its home to its enemies.

At four-fifteen one morning, while Mother Robin was away in search of breakfast, I made a dash and concealed myself in a clump of bushes close to her nest. This contained four babies and was on a low limb of a tree in a mountain apple orchard.

In order to avoid attention, I had enveloped myself in a robe of leafy willows. On her return, one glimpse satisfied Mother Robin that there was a monster concealed in the bushes, and she promptly proclaimed the fact with loud outcries and much ado. The robin is ever borrowing trouble, is a natural alarmist, and no other bird so frequently and so loudly predicts dire events that never come to pass. But this time her distress calls brought a numerous variety of feathered neighbors who were eager to assist or defend. With a noisy uproar of mingled cries of fear, anger, and resentment the birds dashed and whirled about. An occasional bird darted heroically and fiercely at my willowy head in desperate attempts to put me to flight. I remained motionless and silent. Presently they quieted down, and one by one took themselves off.

Her mate did not appear, and Mother Robin calmed herself. After a few minutes of suspicious watching she heeded the insistent calls of the children and brought the first bite to the nest at five-thirty-two.

She rapidly served breakfast. This was obtained from a garden within a stone's throw of the nest. The first course consisted of cut-worms, usually two at a time, an occasional tangle of angle-worms, and a scattering of grasshoppers, with beetles and numerous larvæ that were not identified.

Frequently she paused and with angry 'tut-tut' and 'phit-phit-phit,' together with 'I-know-you-are-there' looks, tried to get me to move. Crawling ants were more nearly effective, but I held the bush for six hours without a move. During this time the baby robins received one hundred and three helpings. After all this food, in a brief inter-mission — during which the mother stared, too astonished even to chatter, at a sheaf of willows waddling across the orchard — the youngsters commenced squalling for something more to eat.

I have often handled baby birds after gaining the confidence of their parents. A male warbler climbed all over me, watching eagerly my handling of his four baby children. Finally, becoming concerned, he pleaded in his way for their release.

What an interesting baby-show young birds would make! Many closely resemble their parents, while others take a season or longer to develop adult plumage. While even the youngsters have pronounced traits of character, these are more noticeable in some species than in others. The baby robin is a masterful fellow, the Baltimore oriole a cry-baby, the thrush baby is patient, calm, and winning, while the little bluebirds are the darlings of all — chubby little midgets.

A wren family by my cabin in the mountains afforded me many pleasant hours. One day a heavy fog prevailed, and the babies went on less than half rations, despite the activity of the dutiful mother. I formed the erroneous conclusion that the fog prevented her from seeing and thus catching the insects, but in all probability it was because all flying insects were under cover. On this foggy, misty day not a single flying insect came to the babies except some flies that were caught inside my cabin. The scanty food consisted of a few flies and a number of grubs and larvæ that I could not identify. The eight youngsters went hungry. Despite this, each bird twice refused to swallow a black beetle, the identity of which was undetermined; and once each in turn refused a brown beetle, much to the bewilderment of the little mother, who stayed by the nest for a number of seconds holding it in her bill. At last she left it on the edge of the nest, but it was never eaten. This was the first instance I had seen of youngsters refusing to eat anything that the mother brought. At this time the birds were about three-fourths grown.

One cold winter day at my mountain home I discovered a new way in which to attract birds. It had been stormy and snowy for some time. For three days everything that the birds commonly depended on for food had been snow-covered, and this, along with the bitter cold, was very severe on the birds. I supplied them with an abundance of food on my south porch. At this altitude, nine thousand feet, there were not many winter birds, but among the callers that came to dine with me were Clark crows, long-crested jays, gray jays, snow buntings, juncos, and, of course, the dear little chickadees.

It was very cold, and in order to keep the drinking-water which I put out for them from freezing, I usually warmed it. This probably was agreeable to the birds. Noticing that one little chickadee lingered on the edge of the dish with great satisfaction, it occurred to me that perhaps

GRAY-HEADED JUNCOS

he was cold, especially his feet. Not having any regulation hot-water bottles, I filled several empty pop bottles which summer tourists had left on a near-by camp-site, corked them securely, and left them on the porch in a line near the food.

These hot-water bottles had not been there long until a junco noticed one of them. Lighting upon it, he gave two or three little twitters of satisfaction, squatted contentedly, tucked his head under his feathers, and in a moment was asleep.

A moment later, on either side of him, were little chickadees. They, too, gave chirps of satisfaction, squatted, and went to sleep. It was not long before the line of bottles was almost covered with sleeping, contented birds, and they aroused a curious interest in Scotch, my dog, who lay near them. He probably watched this unusual gathering with as much surprise and satisfaction as I did from the window just inside.

A BIRD IN THE BUSH

A BIRD IN THE BUSH

It was a dull day for a Tennessee boy who was weeding the field alone. Occasionally he stopped work to wish that the hoe-handle was a fishing-pole. It was hot, and forty times he thought of the swimming-hole. But there were a million weeds between his row and the river.

That evening for excitement he shot a dove. Within a few hours this bird had devoured more than eight thousand weed seeds. The following morning he returned sadly to the hoeing and never dreamed that bird-slaughter had anything to do with the number of times that he could not go fishing.

Every farmer is compelled to board, free of charge, countless mice, insects, weeds, and other destructive pests. But these constant pests are preyed upon by birds who work for him every day without supervision, who never go on a strike, and who board themselves. If these useful birds are killed, the hungry and pestiferous boarders will multiply and almost eat the farmer out of house and home. Most farmers appreciate the value of birds, but unfortunately many gunners and legislators do not.

These pests have the habit of multiplying with amazing rapidity. One weed this year may bring forth one hundred thousand weeds next year. In two years a pair of mice may have fifty pairs of descendants. Among insects, there are many kinds, a single pair of which is capable of multiplying to a million or more in one year! There is no race suicide among pests. Birds are hearty eaters, and it is well to have them about in large numbers, that they may eat the original pairs, or pest capital, and thus keep a constant check upon these insatiable hordes.

From three to four thousand small insects or insect eggs are frequently found in the stomach of a bird. Among the most valuable of insect-eaters are the grosbeaks. The rose-breasted grosbeak once kept the potato-beetle from conquering the potato land of America. The story of this bird during the last generation is of most romantic interest.

During the eighteen-seventies the rose-breasted grosbeak developed a liking for the Colorado potato-beetle, and in a short time was eating these beetles in such numbers that it came to be called 'the potato-bug bird.' At that time the beetle was waging what appears to have been his first war of conquest.

The original home of the Colorado potato-beetle was in the Rocky Mountains of the United States and Mexico. In the good old days he lived almost exclusively upon the sandbur, a relative of the potato. The introduction of potatoes into the old beetle haunts supplied him with a new food that was greatly to his liking. With this he multiplied rapidly, and he early set forth to forage and to feast in all the potato-fields of the earth. His conquering hordes swept successfully eastward, constantly multiplying, causing consternation to the potato-growers and doing enormous damage.

The fecundity of the potato-beetle is beyond belief. The larvæ go through all transformations within fifty days. A single pair of unmolested beetles should, in a single season, have sixty million descendants!

Apparently from six to ten all-conquering years elapsed for the beetle before the grosbeak concentrated his attention upon the invader. Then he commenced to frequent the potato-patch, where he fed upon beetles in all stages of development. Young grosbeaks simply clamored for beetle larvæ, and the new food habit of the grosbeak cleared numerous potato-patches — much to the satisfaction of the early settlers. I have known of parent grosbeaks to transfer upward of a thousand young, soft beetles from potato-hills to the waiting mouths of young grosbeaks in a single day. They also eat other beetles, grasshoppers, cankerworms, gypsy and brown-tailed moths, chinchbugs, army-worms, grubs, the seeds of bindweed, foxtail, and smartweed, weevils that infest forest and fruit trees, and the deadly scale that ruins so many pear, cherry, plum, and apple trees.

The grosbeak is one of the few species of birds which show a distinct increase in population during the last two decades. Abundant food and increased friendliness from man probably account for this increase. Most species, in this period, have suffered a marked decrease in numbers. The passenger pigeon numbered millions when the grosbeak commenced to eat beetles. The pigeon is now extinct.

The rose-breasted grosbeak deserves to be more

generally known and is worthy of a larger place in our literature. Audubon, a century ago, paid a tribute to its musical charms and its good manners. It is almost an ideal bird. It is both useful and beautiful, it is a sweet singer and a member of one of the noblest families in the bird world. It is closely related to the cardinal, and has many striking characteristics.

Its range extends over the vast Mississippi valley into southern Canada. Mrs. Grosbeak is neatly, soberly dressed in buff, gray, and brown. Mr. Grosbeak is handsomely dressed in black and white; a beautiful block of rose brightens his breast, and rose tints the lining of his wings.

Estimates of the Department of Agriculture show that the annual insect damage to crops is from ten to fifty per cent of the crop. Orchards and gardens suffer an average damage of twenty per cent. The average damage to field crops is about ten per cent. In one year, the insects and rat, mice, rabbit, and other animal pests, damaged the growing crops of the United States one billion dollars, and weeds another billion.

Birds will increase the yield of field and orchard if allowed to live there. They are steadily devouring and reducing the multitude of destroyers in the productive areas. Annually they consume trainloads of caterpillars, weevils, beetles, weed seeds, mice, and rats. By being so highly beneficial, birds add measurably to the productivity of the land and reduce the high cost of living.

Every one knows the meadowlark with its eager song and 'breast of buttercups.' It is of high value to the farmer, not so much on account of the weed seed which it destroys as because of the insects which it devours. It feeds to a great extent on chinch-bugs, cutworms, and other insects so injurious to the food products of the farm.

The flicker, too, is a very useful bird, and as many as three thousand ants and one thousand chinch-bugs have been found at one time in a flicker's stomach. But as hearty as even the old birds are, their appetites are small compared with those of their young. Young birds grow rapidly, and young birds, like young boys, seem to be ever hungry.

Birds lead a very active life. Their hearts beat rapidly, and they develop enormous quantities of energy in a short time. They are hearty feeders and digest food speedily. Most parent birds are good providers, and many young birds daily devour their own weight of food. No boy can equal this!

A majority of mated birds raise two broods annually, of five each. The young birds, together with the old ones, each eat approximately one hundred insects a day. Other species of birds live almost entirely upon weed seed, and these require a few trainloads of food annually. Birds whose principal food consists of rats, mice, and rabbits, such as owls and hawks, eat a yearly tonnage that is beyond belief.

Bob-white is one of the most useful of our bird friends. Although an omnivorous and hearty feeder, he eats nothing that man wants and fortunately feeds on the pests of the farmer. In summer he confines his food almost entirely to active chinchbugs, grasshoppers, beetles, and worms. A thousand chinch-bugs a day for each quail is not uncommon.

During winter he begins the work of weedprevention by devouring weed seed. It is estimated that the quail of Virginia consume five hundred tons of weed seed each winter. The killing of quail in winter adds to the cost of farming in summer. The presence of the quail is singularly pleasant and his call is hope-filled and cheery.

Some years ago Dr. Judd, of the Department of Agriculture, calculated that the tree sparrows annually consumed eight hundred and seventy-five tons of weed seed within the bounds of Iowa. Every one is familiar with the habits of the goldfinch — feeding off dandelion and other pestiferous weeds. The dove is an excellent weed-preventer, for it feeds off many seeds of microscopic size and frequently eats several thousand seeds for a single meal.

Weeds that have made life miserable for the farmer, through their fecundity, aggressiveness, and a kind of devilish immortality, are crabgrass, thistles, sorrel, bindweed, ragweed, amaranth, lambs-quarter, and dandelion. There are a few dozen species of birds that live almost exclusively on weed seed.

Among the birds that drive terror to the insects in the garden, are wrens, robins, bluebirds, and vireos. I counted one day one hundred and thirty-four trips within seven hours that a mother wren made from a garden to her nest wherein

THE WESTERN NIGHTHAWK

were wren babies. With one bird ridding the earth of so many insects in such a short time, the numbers of insects destroyed by the birds on a square mile or several square miles would be simply enormous.

Swallows, phœbes, nighthawks, and kingbirds feed freely on many annoying and plaguing insects, pursuing them relentlessly through the air. In the realm of flies and mosquitoes they are terrors.

One of the most amazing and peculiar incidents of bird-killing that has come under my observation, occurred in the outskirts of a city one evening. The local gun club had a shooting contest at passing wild birds. The gunners had their hats off and this revealed the fact that all but two were bald. The birds they were so energetically killing were nighthawks — birds that daily devour scores of flies, gnats, mosquitoes, flying ants, and other irritating, germ-carrying pests that annoy the bald-headed man.

The vagabond crow has many cunning and curious ways. His winning manner and his love for crowds and noise make him a most interesting fellow to watch. His reputation is very bad, but as a matter of fact, he is not as black as he is painted, nor as his color would indicate. On the whole, I think he does more good than harm. He is very fond of mice — which gnaw trees and injure grain and garden — and often feeds upon grasshoppers. There is no denying that he does a great deal of harm; but as a bird for study, few will interest one so much as our sable friend, the crow.

Ofttimes the damage done by otherwise useful birds may be lessened at trifling expense. Corn may be tarred so that crows will not uproot it. As they feed freely upon mice and grasshoppers, it is bad policy to shoot them. A few yards of netting around the poultry-yard will direct hawks and owls to feed upon mice and rabbits. A little study of the habits of birds will enable us to give them the attention that they need if we are to get from them the least harm and the most good.

In 1753 Benjamin Franklin wrote Peter Collinson a letter discouraging the killing of birds thought to be not worth their food. He said: 'Whenever we attempt to... interfere with the government of the world, we have need to be very circumspect, lest we do more harm than good. In New England they once thought blackbirds useless and mischievous to the corn. They made efforts to destroy them. The consequence was, the blackbirds were diminished; but a kind of worm which devoured the grass, and which the blackbirds used to feed on, increased prodigiously; then finding their loss in grass much greater than their saving in corn, they wished again for their blackbirds.'

While almost every species of bird performs a very useful service in the economy of nature, each species fulfills a certain need that cannot well be accomplished by the other species. In other words, each particular species specializes in its work and usually does it well.

The downy woodpecker should be rated as our most useful bird, although looked upon with suspicion by some. He often kills and eats one hundred caterpillars in a day. Of course, he could not consume the entire caterpillar. He eats only the choicest cuts, but to secure these he kills the caterpillar. All woodpeckers render a high economic service in their effective warfare upon tree-destroying insects. Fortunate the orchard-owner whose trees are well cared for by the distinguished woodpecker family.

The quantity of food devoured by insects is large — beyond comprehension. The daily supply for a caterpillar is twice his own weight. Suppose a horse ate proportionately! The larvæ of many kinds of insects daily consume from ten to two hundred times their own weight. Imagine a twenty-pound baby eating a ton of food daily!

It is commonly believed that birds as a whole are quite detrimental to the fruit-grower. Nothing could be farther from the truth. Wrens, robins, and thrushes devour insects by the wholesale in the orchards and gardens.

The presence of a goodly supply of birds in an orchard always means for that orchard more trees and a better quality of fruit, but whenever the birds are scarce, so numerous do the insects become that they not only injure the trees, but ofttimes take possession of much of the fruit. Which would you prefer? to have the worms which infest the orchard in the birds, or in the fruit? If the birds are there, they will stow away most of the worms; but if they are not, the worms will stow themselves away in the fruit.

It is true that on some occasions the loss of fruit caused by robins, thrushes, and other birds amounts to a considerable sum. But the depredations are not regular, and as a rule occur only when the common supply of food upon which these birds live is scarce. And even then, if a fair estimate were placed upon the good work they do and compared with the harm, it would be found that instead of being detrimental to us, they are a source of profit.

Birds are very fond of fruit and especially wild fruit and berries. As a rule they will not eat tame berries if wild ones can be had. So we could use birds for our benefit and prevent their damage simply by providing them with boarding-houses where wild fruit and berries could be had. They are especially fond of choke-cherries, elderberries, strawberries, bittersweet, dogwood, Virginia creeper, blueberries, cedar berries, barberries, juniper, wild grapes, holly, hawthorne, huckleberries, sarsaparilla, and mulberries.

Birds that serve us along the shores of streams and pond, in swamps, on hilltops, in the fields and forest, have abundance of excuse for living even if they did not cheer us with their beauty and their hopeful songs.

If we are to have increased numbers of birds,

we must take measures to attract them and protect them, by providing places where they will be in the least possible danger and where they will have abundance of food. Many scraps of food that now go to worthless dogs and more worthless cats could be fed to the birds. Why not spread a table with scraps of food for our bird friends? In winter suet, old bones, and scraps of meat can be tied to the limbs of trees. When other food is not obtainable, birds can thus subsist and tide themselves over the stormy periods.

Along with the food that we spread and the places of safety that we provide, it would be well, if water is not abundant, to see that they have water to drink and, in addition, a basin of water in which to bathe.

It would be helpful to the general welfare if birds were to have the attention in the way of protection, food, and water, that is given to poultry. The more severely birds have to fight for existence, the less useful service will they give us. Horses and poultry must be fed; in fact, their value largely depends upon the care that is given them. While they need constant feeding, birds need it only in emergencies. If birds were fed through storms and protected from their enemies, they would be with us in checking insect outbreaks — if, indeed, they did not prevent them.

Among the enemies of birds that are making their lives miserable and their numbers fewer, are people with guns, extensive forest fires, and an unnecessary number of useless cats. It would be well for us and our feathered helpers if there were a heavy tax placed upon cats. Probably ninety per cent of the cats that inhabit this country are not only of no value, but an actual source of danger in carrying disease germs. This is not a mere shallow statement, but can be verified by physicians in all parts of the country.

Many cats are poorly fed, and in the nature of things they will prey upon the first object of food they find. Birds are toothsome morsels and will be eaten in preference to mice. Many house cats, even though well fed, will catch and kill birds just for the love of it, influenced, I suppose, by old habits.

Mr. E. H. Forbush,[1] State Ornithologist of Massachusetts, made an intensive study of cats in their relation to birds, carried on over more

[1] Mr. Forbush died March 7, 1929.

than thirty years. It was his conclusion that the cats' chief damage to bird life was in their destruction of the young birds — fledglings — while yet in the nest or just after leaving it and before flying well. He was most positive that a cat would destroy on an average of fifty young birds a season, mostly killed in the nest.

Birds are recognized as of inestimable value to the farmer, who has been called the only necessary man. They seem to have dedicated their lives to the task of keeping this world productive, making it comfortable, and allowing it to remain beautiful. They are Mother Nature's soldiers, incessantly, faithfully, and cheerfully battling day and night the enemies of man.

The pioneers could depend upon wild products for subsistence. But today we cannot rely on these unreliable wild sources. We must domesticate and improve the plants and animals that we find useful. Many things have been domesticated, but we are just beginning to give thought and attention to the care of our most useful wild friends, and these are the birds.

It is probable that in the near future, the beautiful birds that bless us with their good cheer, and that save us so much by their useful services, will be fully appreciated and so kindly treated that every bird that lives will trustfully sit upon our shoulder or eat from our hand.

The supply is not equal to the demand — our need. Many kinds of birds are rapidly diminishing in numbers while insects and weeds continue to multiply. It would pay to have more birds; and we may have more, by leaving groves and thickets for homes and breeding-places, by teaching economic ornithology, and by interesting children in birds.

Small local bird-preserves are needed all over the country, in which birds may receive special attention as well as protection at all times. These would be profitable as well as pleasurable experiment stations. A bird in the bush is worth a dozen in the hand.

THE ADVENTURES OF A TREE

THE ADVENTURES OF A TREE

AN aspen that stood near my cabin had experiences and adventures enough to fill a book. It was one of a grove near a beaver pond that I often visited to watch the interesting activities in beaver world.

One day a beaver left the brook and waddled over as though to cut the tree down. At that time beaver worked in the daytime. They do so no more. Unsympathetic settlers have made it unwise for them to show themselves. Aspen bark is the favorite food of the beaver. He took a bite, chewed it a little, then spit it out. He returned to the brook and went on upstream. Aspen and beaver are found around the world together. The aspen is easily cut and has thick juicy bark which furnishes the beaver most of its food. A green aspen sinks in a short time after being placed in water. Then, too, the aspen grows in wet places close to beaver houses, and when it is cut down the stump sprouts and rapidly grows another tree. Perhaps a majority of all beaver houses in the United States and Canada are of aspen, and I have seen dozens in Alaska that were of aspen sticks.

Across a large lake in the Sawtooth Mountains of Idaho I started on a raft of green aspen logs. The beavers had just felled them and had cut off the tops and small limbs, leaving numbers of small logs ten and twelve feet long. With willows I tied them into a raft, and on this I started to cross. Three miles out in the lake I discovered that green aspen quickly waterlog and sink.

I had not before paid particular attention to this aspen by the brook, but now I stopped and looked it over. Its appearance was good, but when I tapped the trunk with a piece of wood, it did not ring as a sound tree should. It was diseased. I suppose the flavor of the bark did not please the beaver. He did not come back, and the tree lived on.

One day as I passed I saw an excited chipmunk dodging around the aspen trunk, trying to avoid the angry stabs of a robin. Her nest up in the forks had four eggs in it. The chipmunk was the small 'busy' species. He probably had been playing in the treetop with no evil intentions toward the robin's eggs. But the angry cries of

Mother Robin attracted other robins, and all darted at the chipmunk to drive him back into the treetop. I hastened to his rescue. Two of the birds excitedly darted at me. The chipmunk ran down the trunk and when four feet from the ground leaped off and took refuge in a willow-clump by the brook.

I saw the mother robin bring off her four children in safety from this aspen nest. The next summer she returned, repaired the old nest, and in it raised another family. At noon one day a rabbit came hopping along, bit off a small aspen sprout, backed up against the aspen, and began to eat. Mother Robin darted at him, shouting to all the birds within hearing that a monster was in the neighborhood. The rabbit, not liking all this fuss and attention, ran off.

Every tree has an adventurous life and sees many interesting exhibitions of bird and animal life. The Big Trees in California that have lived for from one thousand to five thousand years must have seen every bird and animal in the locality playing or making its escape from an enemy. A few of the Big Trees were old, were flying evergreen flags, when the oldest nation now on earth put up its flag. They are among the largest and tallest of trees, measuring from fifteen to twenty-five feet in diameter and from two hundred to three hundred feet high; a few are even larger.

The aspen is a comparatively small tree. The one by the beaver pond that I visited frequently was of average size and ordinary appearance. It measured eight inches in diameter four feet above the ground and was thirty-five feet high. Its limbs were all on the upper third of the trunk, and from four to six feet long. The tallest aspen I have measured was one on the Tongue Mesa in the Rockies, in an imposing aspen forest. It was one hundred and thirty-five feet high and twenty-two inches in diameter, and it was seventy feet up to the first limb. Its bark was about the color of white birch, but the usual color of the aspen is greenish white. The trunk, except in old trees, is perfectly smooth.

Early each spring before the leaves appeared the aspen bloomed. The blooming of the aspen comes in May in my locality, though a few thousand feet down the mountain-side the aspen blooms two or three weeks earlier. It was as thickly

AN ASPEN GROVE IN THE SAN JUAN MOUNTAINS OF
COLORADO

hung with bloom as it was in summer with its dress of leaves. Long, reddish-brown catkins hung over the limb-ends.

By the brook among the willows were a number of alders and black birches that also bloomed early. On a dry ridge about fifty feet away was a Western yellow pine that bloomed in May. Every tree blooms. The pines and spruces of the mountains have brightly colored blossoms which, though most unlike the bloom of the plum or the cherry, are equally beautiful. Not more than twenty feet from the aspen was a lodgepole pine. Its bloom came in June, and for several days afterwards when the wind blew it sifted the air full of greenish-yellow pollen. Another tree near enough to be called a neighbor of the aspen was a Douglas spruce, one of the tallest and toughest of trees. It bloomed in May and had a beautiful scarlet-ruby jewel bloom.

The earliest bloomer that I have seen is the famous Big Tree. It often blooms when the earth around is deeply snow-covered. The witch-hazel waits until all the other trees have finished blooming and most of them have scattered their seeds. Then, usually in October, when many trees are in colored leaves, it comes out in yellow blossom.

An aspen may be a male or a female. In some species of trees, both the staminate and the pistillate flowers are on the same tree, but commonly the fertilizing pollen comes from another tree. The tree bloom, as well as the bloom of any plant, must be pollinated in order to develop into a seed. Wind carries the pollen for most trees. The fascinating and strange story of pollination is of interest in itself.

The aspen is probably both wind- and insect-pollinated, the pistillate and staminate flowers being on different trees. Like the willows, it attracts the early bees for the wax. Robins and finches, too, and many flocks of north-bound birds alighted to eat these catkins. But not all were eaten. By and by, tiny wisps of cotton, each carrying a fragile seed, floated off, sometimes miles. They filled the four winds thick as snow-flakes. While the seed was being scattered the quivering, light-green leaves came out.

Most species of trees have winged seeds, or seeds that travel by some model of airplane. The aspen has a cotton one, the linden, or basswood, a big monoplane which carries a whole cargo of adventurous seeds hanging below. The pines, spruces, and firs have seeds that fly with one wing. Without a strong wind they do not get far, but they get somewhere, and on an autumn day the entire sky above a coniferous forest appears to be their flying field and is filled with all kinds of flyers. There are dips, somersaults, spirals, and nose-dives, often a thousand at once.

The majority of trees bear seeds each year, but most pines and spruces take two years to mature their seeds, and many fir trees produce seeds only every third year. The lodgepole pine, one of the most interesting of trees, often hangs onto its seeds for many years before scattering them.

The aspen is a rapid grower, and like most kinds of broad-leaf — deciduous — trees, will sprout from the stump or roots. A coyote, in digging for a chipmunk several feet beyond where this aspen was standing, uncovered a part of its roots. There were five little aspen trees, about a foot apart, growing from this root. Out at the end of the root was an aspen fully fifteen feet high. This had also sent out roots and on one of them three young trees were growing. The aspen and the willow do not depend much upon seeds but mostly on sprouts for a start in life.

The aspen is one of the cottonwood-poplar family and is the most widely distributed tree on the globe. It is found in most of the States of the Union. I have seen it at twelve thousand feet above sea-level, where it was a tiny tree that one could hide completely in a hat, and I have seen thousands of aspen at sea-level in the Far North. They are to be found in many places in Europe and Asia and are common in Canada.

Each tree species needs more or less heat and moisture than some other. The orange tree thrives in the warm, moist lands where frost never comes. Other trees, like some of the spruces, grow only on high mountains and in the edge of the Eskimo land. The cactus, the mesquit, and sage-brush grow where conditions are extremely dry, while the willow is ever near water. A species may be able to live in a variety of conditions, but it shows best results where the temperature and moisture suit its needs.

The aspen likes sunshine on its head and moist soil on its feet. Small aspens standing near the water suggest a number of barelegged children.

ENOS A. MILLS EXAMINING CONES IN A
TIMBER-LINE TREE

Also childlike are their lively, playing leaves. Ever on the move, these leaves are jumping, shaking, dancing, clapping, and appear happy all day long.

Many legends have tried to explain why the aspen leaf trembles. Any one who looks closely at the leaf and stem will see for himself. The leaf-stem is thin and flat and turned on edge; the leaf is flat, heavy, and horizontal to the stem. A mere breath or touch tips the leaf right and left; it bobs up and down, plays back and forth, because the vertical flat stem welded onto a horizontal leaf makes a springy combination.

The aspen demands light, it cannot thrive in the shade of other trees. But commonly aspen stands are not crowded, and the grove where my aspen stood was a luxuriant wild garden. Green grass flourished and tall wild flowers crowded in brilliant bloom among the light green trunks. Columbine, blue gentian, white Mariposa lilies, Indian paint-brush, wild pink geranium, and fireweed gave color throughout the summer. Hummingbirds and honey-bees buzzed on busy wings, and silken butterflies sailed on painted ones.

The third summer that I watched my aspen a

hummingbird built a dainty nest in it. I had not seen it until one day a little chipmunk came squealing out from the limbs with a bright-colored object darting for him. This hummingbird did not seem much larger than a bumble-bee, and I am certain that the chipmunk found it even more stimulating than a bee.

The hummingbird's nest was a tiny work of art. Exquisitely decorated and lined, it was a gem. The hummingbird itself was almost a marvel; a tiny bit of burnished life, and yet each year it migrated thousands of miles from its winter home to nest in these scenes, or farther north.

With its long, slender bill, the hummingbird looked like a tiny spear with wings behind. While I stood close one day, this hummer fed her two babies. The long bill was inserted into the mouth of the youngster and moved up and down. It appeared as though she were stabbing the baby; or, as some one has said, more like murder than a dinner-party. But a little later the youngsters were alive and wanted more of it.

Each autumn around the world in the northern zones, the aspen shows its glorious groves of yellow. When the beaver near me assembled around the old home, repairing house and dam and gathering harvest for winter, while the birds went by for southland, the aspen and the willow by the water wore their robes of gold. Oh, that every life might end as gloriously as an autumn leaf!

One autumn day while crossing a desert in Nevada, I stood thirsty by a dry spring, planning how I could reach water most speedily. Glancing up the steep mountain slope I saw in a fine forest two thousand feet above me, a bright spot, a little aspen grove. Probably a tiny stream or spring was near. Two hours later with mouth and tongue badly swollen from dust and thirst, I was drinking from a trickle of clear, cold water to which the aspen had signaled with flag of gold.

The fairy stories say that frost colors the leaves. But if you will watch any autumn you will see that nearly every colored leaf, and the red-cheeked apples, are ripened before frost comes; and that nearly every green leaf that is nipped by frost drops off quickly without color, or becomes black.

A falling tree one day smashed several limbs off the aspen and tore a chunk of bark out of its side. A few inches more into the top would have crushed it to the earth.

That spring I found numbers of beetles working beneath the bark of the aspen where it had been injured by the falling tree. Woodpeckers came daily to peck small holes in the bark and to spear their barbed pointed tongues into the beetle.

Though an aggressive tree in extending its holdings, the aspen is short-lived. Many mature in less than fifty years, and rarely, I think, do they live as long as one hundred years. If favorably situated and if it does not meet with misfortune, one may live to be one hundred and fifty years old. Oaks often live two hundred years, and pines and spruces four or five hundred.

The seedlings of most species of trees cannot grow in the wind and bright sunshine. If they are not sheltered and shaded for a few years they are likely to die. But after they get a start they do better by having the sunlight. The aspen, however, is what may be called a pioneer tree. It is one of the first to appear after a forest fire or something else has cleared the ground. Pioneer trees are greatly needed, like pioneer people, to form first settlements, to get things started. Afterwards, there are numbers of worthy people who do not care for pioneer life, who will come along and do work just as hard, but, I believe not so interesting.

There are more than five hundred species of trees in North America, but only about twenty of these should I call pioneers. There are many that are near-pioneers; but the majority of trees — oaks, pines, spruces, and scores of other long-lived and useful trees — for best results need to have the pioneering work done for them.

Among the other interesting pioneer trees that I know, besides the aspen, first of all is the lodge-pole pine, then the alder, birch, jack pine, red-wood, some species of maple, and most of the cottonwoods and willows. An old-field pine in the South, and the famous white pine in the North are ever ready to do pioneering. Commonly the pioneer type of tree can adapt itself to more kinds of places than other species.

The old pine on a ridge near the aspen had a big charred place between two big roots. Here it had been burned long ago. How long ago? One windy night another Western yellow pine behind it blew over, and in the stump of this, which I sawed off and split to pieces, I found a fire-scar sixty-three annual rings deep inside the bark. With a chisel I cut a small chunk out of the old scar on the other pine, and this revealed a charred place beginning with the sixty-third annual ring inside the bark. I bored into the bottom of a near-by lodgepole, and it was sixty-two years old — it had sixty-two annual rings. So there must have been a fire here sixty-three years before. This had burned almost everything but the willows in the edge of the water and the thick-barked pines.

Aspens, lodgepoles, and other pioneer trees commonly sprout up the year following a fire, and I thought that probably the aspen, when I could get a count on its rings, would show sixty-two. It was probable that the lodgepole and the few other middle-aged aspens and other lodgepoles growing here had started from seeds blown onto the burned area immediately after a fire. This fire, I should guess, had started from lightning, but it may have been from an Indian's camp-fire.

In the 'Story of a Thousand-Year Pine,' I tell of a tree that lived more than a thousand years and of the experiences it had. After it was down, with the help of two men, I learned its history as told in the annual rings. It was the most interesting of the trees I have examined.

The aspen finally died, probably from beetles working under the bark and other tree-killers working in the roots. I had planned to cut it down as soon as it died and count its annual rings and also try to determine what had killed it.

But that spring a pair of woodpeckers made a nest in its trunk. The tree was just to their liking for cutting and chiseling, being soft wood and fairly dried out, and of the common size used by woodpeckers. I thought the tree would probably still be useful for some time.

And so it was. As soon as the three woodpecker babies were out of the nest, a little chipmunk took possession. The next summer a bluebird nested in the old woodpecker's hole, and the following summer a fussy pair of house wrens occupied it. Another year a pair of woodpeckers again used it.

One winter day I went out to cut the dead aspen down. I had not seen anything occupying the old woodpecker's nest for some time. It was a cold day, and the wind was blowing. The first stroke of my ax, and one, two, three, six, chickadees came rushing out of the hole. This was their winter home. I left the dead aspen standing.

Black bear cubs appear to favor the aspen for climbing practice or gymnastic pranks. The soft bark affords secure clawholds. Once I saw four cubs in the same aspen. A contusion or excrescent scar usually grows over cuts or deep scratches that are made in the bark; this relief growth lasts for years. Hundreds of aspens carry bear-claw and other markings, some of which may have been made a generation ago.

In various scenes and in different nations I have come in contact with the friendly aspen. Many times during my wilderness journeyings the inner bark was my only food for days together. This is tender and juicy; in the spring it has a good flavor. It was eaten raw, roasted, or boiled. Sometimes I spiced it with aspen or other buds, and at times it was combined with berries, nuts or mushrooms.

Aspen wood has many uses. Light and free from splinters, it was much worn by ancient warriors as a buckler. A hot, quick, clean fire-producer, it was the prize fuel of pioneers in many states. Even when green its wood will burn with a little encouragement. Do you know the pungent smell of green-aspen smoke, or the

172

primeval scenes awakened in the imagination by its presence?

Billions of safety-tipped matches are of aspen wood, which is also excellent for high-grade excelsior, and makes fine jet-black charcoal and smooth white paper. Possibly the paper on which this is printed is an incarnation of some aspen. Thus the merry and active aspen, having lived its short life, may become the preserver of records bearing facts and figures, printed or painted flights of fancy, tales of high aspiration and heroic deeds; and under every sun and sky it may be the trusted messenger that carries the divine story — a story as old and ever young as the aspen itself.

Late one winter the aspen blew over. After sawing the stump off just below the earth-level among the root welds, so as to get the full growth, I counted the annual rings — sixty-two. It was sixty-two years old when it died. I sawed across the trunk three feet above the ground and counted only fifty-six rings. It had taken the little aspen six years to grow three feet high. An aspen often grows more rapidly than this. The wood was nearly white with a tinge of yellow. Its grain was straight. I measured an aspen that was nine inches in diameter that had only twenty-one annual rings — that is, was twenty-one years old. But one of the tiny aspen at timber-line, far up the side of Long's Peak, had fifty-six rings and was not yet one inch in diameter.

Some kinds of trees grow faster than other species, but if all conditions are favorable — sunshine, good soil, moisture, and room — any kind will grow rapidly. The Big Trees take about twelve years for each inch of diameter. But in the Rocky Mountains an average for many kinds of trees, from many kinds of places, is ten years for one inch of diameter; that is, on an average, a tree ten inches in diameter would be one hundred years old.

This aspen had a fire-scar on the trunk just above its roots. A camp-fire probably had been built against it. This was when it was twenty-seven years old. The same year some one cut the letter 'M' deeply through the bark, probably some one of this camping-party.

The annual rings are full of the tree's experiences. This annual ring shows the thickness of the wood grown each year; a thin ring shows that

A CRYSTAL-WHITE ALDER

SPRUCE IN THE WINTER WOODS

the year was a hard one — too dry, the soil poor, or the tree too crowded, or possibly that caterpillars or some other pest had hampered growth. If a fire burns through an annual ring the scar will remain in the ring or rings burned, and if the scar is in the fiftieth annual ring, counting from the center — the heart — of the tree, we know that the tree was fifty years old when the fire came.

Trees grow in diameter each year, by putting a coat or wrapping of wood — an annual ring — over trunk, limbs, twigs, and roots, just under the bark. The last annual ring is on the outside. Trees in the torrid zone, where there is no interruption of the growth by cold or other causes, do not have annual rings.

But how do trees grow taller? If a pin be stuck in the bark of a tree, four feet above the earth, and left there five years and the tree grows five feet higher, how high is the pin above the earth? Just four feet. If a limb is just as high as you can reach, the tree may grow twenty feet higher, but you will still be able to touch the limb. A tree does not push up through the ground. It grows taller each year by growing a new top on top of the old one. The top is called the leader.

Each spring the near-by lodgepole sent out limbs like spokes from a wheel, at the very tip-top, and also from the tip-top sent up a shoot or leader fourteen inches high. One winter four feet was broken off the top. The following spring the four limbs in the whorl nearest the top bent upward and raced for leadership. Two of these were distanced and died. The other two ran neck and neck, and as a result the tree had a double top.

An old hunter who was something of a story-teller and who did not know much about trees, took me out into the woods near a cliff where there was a spruce with many limbs upon it. In a crotch between a big limb and the trunk, was the partly overgrown head and a few other bones of a deer. Just how these old bones came to be up there I cannot guess, unless during a flood the high water left them.

But the old hunter's story was, that one day his dog frightened a deer. In jumping high the deer caught in this crotch, which was then about five feet above the earth. He was busy and did not come for the deer until the following day. A lion had so nearly eaten it by that time that he left it in the tree. He said the tree had grown fifteen feet higher since that time and thus had raised the bones to their present height. This was a good story, but no tree ever grew that way.

I sawed off the short section of the aspen tree that contained the woodpecker's nest — the nesting-hole in which baby woodpeckers, bluebirds, and wrens had lived, and in which chipmunks and chickadees and probably mice had slept and taken refuge from snow and rain-storms. Often, when I look at this, I am reminded of the many times I watched it and its wild visitors, when it was glorious with golden leaves, beautiful with white snow flowers, and how at night its leaves whispered when I stood beneath it listening to the merry hoots of a jolly, moon-eyed owl in its top.

GUARDIANS OF THE FOREST

GUARDIANS OF THE FOREST

As we adventure through life we are ever indebted to the trees. Primitive man appreciated trees for fuel, food, and shelter, but civilized man is just beginning to give thought to the importance of the forests. For the order of the earth, for every vista that pleases and for every scene that cheers, we are chiefly indebted to the flowers, the birds, and the trees. These not only make the earth useful to us, but they give to nature those subtle charms which enable us to have and to hold high ideals.

The forests which Mother Nature planted for us in America have contributed enormously to the accumulated wealth now in the United States. Wood and lumber have countless uses. It is estimated that at least one third of our wealth has been drawn from the forests which were here when the pioneers came. Trees are a necessity, and any nation that has allowed her forests to perish has in a short time perished herself.

One of the most impressive facts in all nature

is the relation of the forests to the flow of the streams. Wherever forests are removed from the watersheds, the water rushes off hurriedly and frequently in destructive floods — floods which erode away the soil and which fill the channels of the rivers and harbors of the earth. If we want more springs, more constantly flowing streams, which will cease to go above the high-water mark, we must maintain the forests at their source.

A tree is the most highly organized of plants and is in many ways helpless because it is rooted to the earth. It must stand in one place all its life and bear the good and the harmful things which come to it, and there is a superabundance of harmful things that come to trees.

The moment a baby tree is born it is subject to the deadly attacks of insects and small animals. As a tree begins to spread its tiny arms in the sunlight, as it increases in size, it increases the number of its enemies; so, as a rule, the more aged a tree is, the more enemies it has. As a tree ages, scores of insects make their home upon it and, being parasitic, these insects live by feeding upon the very tree in which they make their home. Of a million seeds possibly one sprouts and starts to grow; and of the ten thousand little trees that start, one may live to old age.

Insects are the worst enemies of trees. The Big Tree is the only species that is not subject to insect attack, which probably accounts for its great antiquity on the earth. There are said to be more than four hundred insects that bite and assail oaks. There are dozens of kinds of beetles, borers, lice, weevils, and other harmful tree pests.

Most trees are killed by small pests working at the roots or getting under the bark. The vital part of the tree is between the inner layer of the bark and the outer layer of the wood. In the vitals is the circulatory system. Girdle a tree by cutting all around the trunk through the bark, and the tree dies.

Fire is another tree enemy. Fossil trees nearly two million years old have been found partly burned. From this and other evidence we may gather that forest fires have afflicted forests for millions of years. What started forest fires so long ago? Red hot lava may start a fire burning, and even ashes from a volcano. Lightning occasionally sets a fire.

Trees have developed means of resisting cold,

heat, drouth, and insect attacks. Old wounds, if not too deep or extensive, are healed over in time, and if a top is broken, new shoots replace it. But millions of trees have died from fire injuries, or through insect enemies getting into the tree's vitals through a cut, hack, or burn in the bark. If something tears off the bark, or breaks a limb, or if a beetle bores through the bark, many kinds of tree-killers will enter through these openings and eat on the vitals of the tree. A fire which burns off part of the bark often opens the way for small parasites or fungi to get into the tree; and even though the bark grows over the wound, these entered enemies remain and years later cause the tree to die.

Why had woodpeckers made eight holes, one above the other, in the trunk of an old pine? None of these holes led to a nest. As I watched a woodpecker making a ninth one, I discovered that the holes, from two to four feet apart, were along a split in the thick bark, which had been caused by lightning. This break through the protecting bark had allowed numbers of destructive insect enemies to reach the vitals of the tree. Woodpeckers, each with a cutting-tool bill, were doing effec-

WESTERN YELLOW PINE

COLORADO BLUE SPRUCE

tive work cleaning out these invading tree enemies. The old pine lived on.

There is a beautiful intimacy between the birds and the trees. The woodpecker, the wood thrush, the owl, the jay, the cardinal, and the dear chickadee appear to be keeping a vow to dress and cheer the tree temples for you and for me. A tree is one of the most valuable, as well as one of the most beautiful, plants that grows. Everywhere that we may hope to live the trees are already there. Irresistible and steadfast, the trees have gone before.

Birds distribute tree and plant life over the globe — scatter seeds and become tree planters. And they wage an incessant war upon the countless insect enemies of trees. Our little friends of the air, who sing as they work, are the chief protectors and perpetuators of our most useful of tree friends. Without birds the forest, through whose sacred and sun-sifted aisles we have come from cave to cottage, would soon perish from the world. Without trees the human race would become a lost child, crying in the night.

More than half of all our birds live in trees and in trees make many kinds of nests. Nests hang

185

from limbs, rest on top of limbs and in forks, and are pecked out of solid wood and worked out of rotten half-hollow limbs. It would be hard on many kinds of useful, happy birds if there were no tree nesting-places.

Although the faithful efforts of birds have not been appreciated, and although their willing wings have often ornamented those whom they would have served, the birds have ever been efficient, and those that remain are still trying to paradise the earth and to keep it enriched with their songs. While birds, perhaps, do the most for us in the ideal world by inspiring us, yet they perform many important services in the world of necessity that cannot be estimated in dollars and cents.

Chickadees, nuthatches, and woodpeckers are the most faithful servants of forests. Some of them, and in many localities all three species, stay with the trees and serve them the year round. Often I have watched the chickadees carefully searching over the twigs and small limbs for wood-lice, caterpillars, ants, and scale. At the same time the nuthatches take good care of the big limbs, frequently walking along the under side like a fly. From time to time as they hunt

over the branches they pry off a piece of bark
with their bills, and in doing so will sometimes
uncover a few thousand insect eggs or surprise a
beetle, which they devour.

While the little birds are busy with the small
limbs, Dr. Woodpecker is giving his attention to
the larger ones, and will be seen walking round
and round the trunk, or going head foremost up
it. Occasionally he will find a beetle too big for
the tiny nuthatch or the little chickadee, and if
you will watch the doctor, you will notice that
he occasionally puts his ear to the bark and
listens; if he hears some ants or borers working
beneath the bark, he at once adjusts himself for
an operation.

Dr. Woodpecker is the chief surgeon of the
forest. Whenever an ant, beetle, or borer gets into
a tree it becomes a source of serious injury. Ofttimes one or all of these insects are the cause of
the tree's losing its life. They are safe from both
the nuthatches and the chickadees, but they are
not beyond the reach of Dr. Woodpecker. Even
though the borers and ants may make very
crooked tunnels in the tree, this does not save
them from capture. Folded within his long bill,

the doctor carries a long, flexible tongue with a barbed point. This he thrusts far into the holes made by the ants and borers, and the ant that comes in contact with his tongue sticks fast to its adhesive surface, while the beetle is impaled upon the point of it, and is drawn wriggling out.

When the trees are very small, they receive much protection from two families of birds, both of which are usually considered as belonging to the criminal class. These are the hawks and the owls. They are the guardians of young trees, the hawks fighting for them in the daytime and the owls defending them when darkness is over the land. Every fruit-grower and tree-planter realizes the enormous amount of damage which rabbits do to young trees, and when it comes to holding rabbits in check, certainly the hawks render us valuable service. Rats and mice eat both the roots and the bark of young trees. Hawks and owls feed extensively on rats, mice, rabbits, and gophers, and there are fifty species of hawks and owls in the United States that prey upon these prolific destroyers.

Hawks are often called chicken thieves, and owls are placed in the same class by some. It is true that some will eat chickens, but they do not all do so. The great horned owl, and the Cooper's and sharp-shinned hawks, are the greatest robbers of hen-roosts, while the other species of hawks and owls rarely bother them. But even taking the worst class of these chicken thieves and balancing the good they do with the loss they occasion us, and it is quite probable that they are more useful than detrimental.

From time to time in the past, some State has offered a bounty on hawks, yet there is no doubt, from an economic standpoint, but this has been very detrimental to the general welfare. The killing of hawks has allowed the number of rats, rabbits, field mice, and gophers to increase. Rats are filthy and spread disease; in many localities they are so active that poultry-raising is not profitable. As these animals increase, they must have something to live on, and since much of their living comes from food-supplies needed by man, their increase occasions our loss.

During a recent mouse plague in Nevada, one investigator estimated that there were about ten thousand mice per acre. In this district the same investigator counted in one day twenty-seven hawks and a number of owls hanging dead upon wire fences — the exhibits of ignorant gunners. A hawk or an owl will devour on an average three mice a day.

The game-keepers of the Scotch moors at one time so watchfully killed off hawks and birds of prey that the weak and sickly grouse disseminated distemper and probably caused more harm than the hawks.

There are more than twelve hundred kinds of North American birds. The lives of most of these birds are almost entirely beneficial to us. Of course there are a few birds, as there are a few people, whose existence as a whole is decidedly detrimental; in other words, the world would be richer without them. But there are less than a score that I should place in this class. Among these are the English sparrow, the goshawk, the great horned owl, the Cooper's hawk, the magpie, and our emblematic eagle. During certain periods even the harmful birds are useful. The others are profitable at all times.

We save wealth by saving birds. Whenever the bird population is so small that the birds cannot give proper care to the trees, in a little while the trees suffer greatly or die from the unhindered attacks of insect enemies.

Birds seem to regard the trees as unfortunate big brothers who are from accident so injured and entangled that they cannot fly. They give trees loving care and cheer them with songs, possibly trusting and believing that the trees will sometime be able to fly with them to fairer scenes. How wonderful to have wings! to cover miles of territory to other congenial conditions! Unlike trees, forever rooted to one spot, birds have an unlimited choice of home, may have several homes in the same year.

Here is interdependence of the highest type. For homes and for food, birds return most often to trees or other plants. And for the preservation of the trees and plants we must thank the birds. The cheerful services of birds and the delightful intimacy between the birds and the trees, make one of the sweetest, dearest stories that is lived or learned on nature's loving breast.

Knowing the relation of things in nature is a field of progressive thought; of delightful, continued, and sustained entertainment. Those who are happiest have the greatest number of points of contact with the world, and the field of nature arouses one's power of observation and increases the store of information so that one has broader sympathies.

The study of bird-life is one of the most fascinating of occupations. To observe birds with the idea of finding out their useful qualities is worth while, and to study them for pure delight — for the exercise in the good outdoors and the cheerful tone it gives — is an influence which will better and broaden the life of any one. Bird-study is not always the long list of birds which you have seen or the nests discovered. Be content with little — wait for the birds — still-hunt. Envelop yourself in a hole of silence if you desire to see birds.

There are many things of interest about trees. They have been on earth millions of years, and during this long period of development each species has adapted itself — has become accustomed — to a peculiar environment, one in which another species might not thrive. Several species of trees, with few changes, have been on earth for ages. Fossil redwood trees have been found that appear decidedly like present redwoods; yet the fossils are of trees that lived possibly two million years ago.

Many species of trees have inherited a tendency to twist, and do twist, if they grow in rocky places where their roots wedge among rocks which cannot be split wider apart. I have had the best opportunity to study twisted trees in fire-killed areas where the bark has been burned off, and at timber-line and in other wind-swept places, where the bark has been sand-blasted away. Even lightning is given a spiral journey by the structure of a twisted tree. When lightning strikes a tree of ordinary straight grain, it usually runs directly to earth, plowing a furrow, bark-deep, along the way. But when a twisted tree is struck, the bolt usually follows the spiral fibres round and round the trunk to the ground.

Most species of trees that I have found with a twisted grain, showed a right twist, although I found others twisted to the left. It is almost an impossibility to split these larger twisted trees. Limbs or knots run through the coiled spirals like so many iron bolts or reinforcing rods of steel. The twist runs round and round like the turns of a screw or stripes on candy in the most closely twisted trees, but more often it is that of a much elongated spiral spring, going around a tree of a foot diameter once in every rise of two feet in height.

The most closely twisted trees that I have seen are the species of limber pine (*Pinus flexilis*). These grow in the Rocky Mountains from an altitude of eight thousand feet to timber-line, somewhat above eleven thousand feet. Most people think that the wind is the chief cause of this twisting, but I have found pronounced twists in trees in sheltered coves and in the bottom of windless cañons. Rock resistance appears to be the chief cause of twisted tree growth. I have a photograph of two limber pines which grew side by side in a violently wind-swept place. One of these is twisted, and the other straight-grained. The straight-grained one is standing in deep soil, and the other in shallow, rooted in the cracks of a nearly solid rock.

Birds and trees belong both to economics and to the fine arts. Without birds, the useful, stately trees, which now give us their beauty and their blessing, would wither and die from the attacks of unresisted insect enemies. Exterminate birds,

A TWISTED LIMBER PINE KILLED IN
A FOREST FIRE

A LIMBER PINE THAT SURVIVED A
FOREST FIRE

a well-known French scientist has said, and all the trees will die within seven years. How dreary would be the world if they should perish from the earth! Without either birds or trees there would be little on this earth to love.

I have had great days in the wilds, and I wish I could transfer to you the poetry of the pathless woods, or the raptures wrought by wild lakes with forest frames and shadow-matted shores. Many a strong day I have had with the mists on the mountains, or with the eagles among the snow-edged crags. Intensely I have lived on Alpine moorlands, with groves and tree-fringed grass-plots, with white cascades, with forests green and grand, in silence and in storm, with winter and with summer, and with the shadows of the pines.

Many a summer night I have had my dreams in a forest glade. Here, where the perfume of the flowers mingled with the spice of the pines, I held communion with nature. Here, I listened to the whip-poor-will's song, watched the white and lovely moon, felt the caresses of the air so soft and pure, while echoes died away in the moonlight. Many a night in the wilds I have had rest and reverie by my camp-fire, which blazed a bloom of glory in the forest black and still. All mortals seem strangely influenced while facing a fire in the woods. I wonder why the camp-fire, with its wild and strange spell, entrances, calms, charms, or arouses the mind like music. I would that words could tell the thoughts that arise in me as I sit by a fire in the woods.

Again, in memory, I hear the rhythmic sounds of the never silent woods.

Again a crag and pine cut their ebony outlines on evening's golden sky; again I listen as the wind breaks and booms, pauses and whispers among the mountain pines.

Again I watch the eager ouzel dare the torrent, again I hear his enchanting song as he sits by the white cascade wrapped in spray.

Again the wood thrush charms with marvelous melody in forest depths among the shadows of the pines.

MUSIC OF THE WILDS

MUSIC OF THE WILDS

Go where you will in the Rockies and the birds will greet and cheer you. They will make you feel the spell of living. Peaks, plateaus, snowfields, forests, cañons, meadows, lakes, and streams — each have their busy, happy bird people. A number are mountain residents, others are trailers of the sun. Grace, beauty, and song place them in the world of art. The eagle soars the blue, the ptarmigan and the rosy finch live with Arctic flowers and snow. On and beyond the trail is the confiding 'camp-bird,' the restless hummingbird, the robin that you know, the blackbird with painted wing, the long-crested jay — handsome impersonator, the boisterous nutcracker, the wise magpie, the childlike chickadee, and the bluebird with brilliance of mountain skies. The cheerful, daring water-ouzel sings to its cascading brook, the cañon wren echoes in the mysterious cañon depths, wood-notes wild of hermit thrush charm the forest, and the white-crowned sparrow sings to the night. The inspired solitaire, the matchless songster of timber-line, gives his divine melody to listening pines and crags, mingling his music with the elemental sounds of winds and waters. Bird-songs are a part of the music of existence.

The thrush, the mockingbird, the skylark, and the cañon wren are all celebrated singers. But of all the birds in the West, or in the world, the solitaire is the one most hopefully eloquent in his song. His every note is cheerful and inspiring. The song of the thrush is touched with sadness — brings loneliness and reflection. But that divine singer, the solitaire, is the choir invisible of the forest.

Every one might well spend a day in the elemental scenes above timber-line. Scenery, like music, is thought-compelling. Birds, bees, and butterflies enjoy the glorious sunshine of the heights and find altitude beneficial. With the songs of birds and the hum of insects is mingled the music of ever-falling water, and the intermingling of the sounds and silences of the wild is impressive here as nowhere else.

In these matchless surroundings the solitaire sings. To me his song is the most enchanting melody of nature. It stirs one's heart to the utmost and puts into utterance the glorious harmonies of the heights.

AN ALPINE LAKE, A MEETING-PLACE FOR BIRDS

SUNSET FROM ABOVE THE TIMBER-LINE
When the solitaire sings

By the camp-fire I have heard the call of the wild. Many times I have listened to the leaves in the night and heard the far, faraway waterfall. Often, with coyote's strange cry or the owl's lonely story close to my fading fire, I have fallen asleep encircled by the steadfast trees at timber-line. After long, sweet sleep under the open sky, I have been awakened at breaking dawn by the matchless melody of the solitaire. Hear his notes of peace and hope, and you will feel that Pan is piping in the valley just below and that all is right with the world.

The music of the solitaire stands alone in the realm of bird-song. It sings of the solitudes among the cathedral groves, by dreaming lakes, beneath sunny skies, and up where the world is young. It appeals most strongly when heard at dawn, pouring forth from a crumbling cliff or crag; but when it is heard at evening in the sunset's golden glow, there is a tranquillity about it that rests while it inspires.

Whatever the reason for bird-song, whether it comes from exuberance of spirit or devotion to a mate, it is enough to know and appreciate this music of the wilds. The solitaire, like many other shy, retiring birds, scarcely makes its presence known except through song. And then how gladly, gloriously it breaks the stillness! The listening mate, if to her he sings, must truly be an inspired and inspiring audience. The solitaire's song is entirely his own; it is like no other that I know, and is beyond comparison with any.

While of all birds perhaps the quietest, in dress and in manner, the solitaire deserves to be better known. He chooses the unfrequented places, the open glades near timber-line, where subalpine firs border a stream or lake. His nest is on the ground, in old stumps or among rocks sheltered by matted dwarfed trees. But for his song he flies to the top of some tall dead tree near by, and transforms the elemental beauty of the wilderness into music. In appearance he is not unlike the mockingbird, though smaller — a brownish-gray bird, paler beneath, wings and tail marked with white.

By the alpine lakes and brooks, one may see — usually will see — the water-ouzel, one of the loveliest birds of the West. He is of a bluish slate-color, and, because of his characteristic dipping motion, is also known as the dipper. It has been suggested that his constant bobbing is a protective advantage to him in the environment in which he lives; poised temporarily midstream on a boulder, he is in harmony with the motion of the rising and falling water. In his flight he follows every wind and bend in the stream's course, making every leap that the cascades make, and following the longest curves through which the stream flows.

The ouzel is one of the most interesting and independent of birds. In winter he follows the streams down the mountain-slopes, getting his food from the stream-bed, often under the ice, and spending the nights in nooks between ice and water along the bank. He nests by the water's edge, usually beneath an overhanging bank, or upon a rock ledge jutting under the spray of a waterfall. He likes the swiftest mountain brooks, dashing through the flying spray with no concern.

Of all land birds, he lives the closest to, and spends the most time in, the water, plunging off the boulder's edge into the dashing mountain stream as confidently as taking to the air. The young birds take to the water almost as soon as they leave the nest, having perhaps no alternative, unless to be left perched on some boulder where they chance to light. They are among the most winsome of youngsters, feigning great helplessness in what would look like a sorry plight for any bird, if we did not know its water habits.

In June the water-ouzel pours forth his most melodious song, the very exuberance of bird music. But, unlike most species, he sings every day in the year. So far as I know, the water-ouzel is the only being in the wilderness world that is never in the least discouraged. His days are processions of gladness. He sings while blizzards boom, and also in the perfumed summer air, and never sounds a note of sorrow. He sings for the very joy of living, and there is no season that he does not welcome with a courageous heart. He should be taken as the emblem of every outdoor lover who wants to get the most out of life.

Another bird that I hope every one has heard and will hear again, is the hermit thrush. He sings in solitude. In midday his fluty, silvery tones gently spread and float away through the mellow light of the forest; when twilight falls, his pure, rich melody rings hopefully out on the dying day. The melody of the thrush sounding

A BABY WATER-OUZEL NAPPING BETWEEN FEEDINGS

A MOUNTAIN CHICKADEE

sweetly, soft and low through the dim woods — the ineffable mystery and voice of nature — will purify and elevate the lives of men.

It is a blessing to watch our fellow creatures, especially the birds, when they are in repose and content — speaking to themselves in low, sweet undertones, assurance that this brother bit of life finds joy in living too. How cheerless the out-of-doors would be if the good and useful birds were gone! To gladden the trail of life with song — how sufficient is it for their existence! and the best of reasons for their protection, even if they did no more.

The song of the rose-breasted grosbeak is one of the sweetest. He loves to sing and sings like a lover. Often he enchants the night with a song that is as soft and romantic as moonlight.

Many of the sparrow family are delightful singers. The goldfinch, to me, is bewitching in every note and tone. During nesting-time he is a devoted soloist, who, perched near his home or flying in broad circles around it, pours out his heart in song. It is an exceedingly appealing song, sweet and varied, suggesting a canary's, but still no more like it than a tropical forest is like a hothouse. Whenever he sings there is love, tenderness, and worship in every note. Oh, if the goldfinch were to sing no more it would be sad indeed. Sometime I hope you will go out to see this radiant bird and listen when he says, 'Hear me, hear me, dearie,' that you will stop and hear tones to be matched only by a mother's cradle song, tones which I hope are still like sunshine in your soul.

One dreamy autumn day I lay beneath a piñon pine on the rim of the matchless Grand Cañon of the Colorado. The silence, the magnitude, the strangeness of this cañon — the story of a million years and a day — were eloquently impressive. Cloud shadows moved over its vastness. As I lay looking down into its depth and at its magnificent colors, a cañon wren began to sing.

The bird was somewhere in a niche below, and I could not see the tiny singer. With intensity he sang of all the joys of life. His echoing liquid song carried the strangeness and the spirit of the desert, and seemed to make more vast the vastness of the cañon depths. How often his brave and hopeful song must be lost in the gorge and desert solitudes!

I wondered about the feelings of the Indian when his imagination was stirred by this creative cañon song. Primitive people formerly worshipped birds, and they probably received more consolation from them than we do today. Years ago Indians in the Southwest put up nesting-boxes for the birds. I wish we might know the stirring part that bird-songs through the ages have played in schooling the savage, in giving sympathetic education to primitive man.

When mating birds sang of life's rare joys, many a primitive mother may have paused in her drudgery to listen and to think; many a maiden to dream; and many small boys and girls may have paused in their play to listen and to wonder.

The Piute Indians tell a poetic legend concerning the creation of birds. The Great Spirit, ages ago, in looking down upon the earth as its autumn colors lay glorious in the sunshine, was saddened with the thought that the colored leaves would soon fall to the earth and fade into forgetfulness. At this time birds had not been called into existence. So he concluded to create them out of the colored leaves on the trees. Out of the leaves of the oak he made the robin; out of the yellow leaves of the willow he made the canary. The brilliant red of the maple became the redbird, and each of the birds received a bit of color from the other leaves.

But the bluebird received no color, was dressed in subdued gray. Consequently he ever sought a home in seclusion. While flying high in search of a home he peeped into a hole in the curtain of the sky. Then he concluded to go through to the other side. In getting through the hole he was colored where the sky had rubbed. Mrs. Bluebird at once followed, but she was only faintly touched with blue hue, because he had taken off most of the sky color.

An Iroquois Indian legend is also interesting:

Once the earth was entirely hidden under great waters; there were no islands, no continents. The waves of a shoreless sea rolled round the world. Fishes swam the great sea, and birds, never resting, ever soared the air. In the wide waste of waters there was nothing on which to alight. The birds felt that there was need of a higher intelligence than themselves.

One day the birds in a large congregation were

discoursing on this very matter, when they beheld a lovely woman dropping out of the high, blue sky. They agreed to save her and crowded together with outstretched and overlapping wings. Upon this throbbing, feathery island in the air, the woman landed and lay panting. Lovingly she caressed the wings and kissed the tinted plumage of her bird benefactors.

The large and enduring place which birds have in legend and in literature shows that they have long been a source of helpfulness and hopefulness— that is, of æsthetic value to our race. Shakespeare made over six hundred references to birds and bird-life. Bryant's 'Lines to a Waterfowl' and Shelley's 'Ode to a Skylark' show how inspiring birds are to the mind.

Bird songs reach and help almost every one. When Longfellow says,

'Tis always morning oomewhere,
Somewhere the birds are singing evermore'

he enables us to see sunshine and hear bird-songs round the world.

What had Burroughs received when he gave out these poetic lines?

'Thy voice is like a hermit's reed,
That solitude beguiles;
Again 'tis like a silver bell
Adrift in forest aisles.'

One of the greatest children of nature that the world has produced was that most famous of ornithologists, John James Audubon.

Among the early influences of his life which did so much to mold his character and direct the energy of his eighty years, were walks out with nature with his father, who made it a point to tell him interesting stories concerning the birds that were around. He was allowed to ramble the forests that fringed Paris and was not sent to school until past the age of fifteen.

By this time, the ideal of his life was so developed that it was not to be suppressed. His father and others tried to persuade him to take a military course and become a soldier under Napoleon, whose successes at this time had literally robbed France of its sanity and deluged all Europe with blood.

But Audubon had heard sweeter and more stirring music poured forth by the birds in the mellow-lighted forest aisles than was played by even the military bands of France. Mother Nature had so sweetened his soul that he was not to be intoxicated and misled to go out to kill his brother on war's red and ruined fields. His love for birds and for nature was so great that his father sent him to America to take charge of his estate there. Here came one of the fortunate influences in Audubon's life. He met the daughter of an English neighbor, Lucy Bakewell, who was a great nature-lover. She and Audubon fell in love almost at sight, and through their fifty happy years of wedded life, from time to time she was the only friend he had. Almost every neighbor and associate criticised and condemned them at times for the life that Audubon led.

Most of Audubon's life were years of bitter trial; of struggles that genius so often has with poverty, but at last the triumph came. His book and magnificent drawings were published, and then he had tribute from the honorable and intellectual world. But in the midst of these triumphs, in the midst of all the acclaim that came to him from London, Edinburgh, and Paris, he sailed away from the Old World to America, to see his wife and children, whom he still felt were 'his heart's best treasures.'

It is impossible to estimate the profound benefit which the world through all the years will receive from this gentle, patient man, this bird-loving genius. I believe that the golden age is coming, and I believe that some day the birds will build their nests in every cañon that is now desolate of life.

So long as the birds continue to sing — and they will sing wherever they are allowed to live — so long as the mockingbird pours forth its marvelous melody in the balmy air of the South, the robin and the meadowlark sing to the cottage — just so long shall we continue to reverence and honor the good, great Audubon, and the patient, loving woman who helped him to do his wondrous work of saving to mankind the blessings of the birds and their music for evermore.

THE BIG AMERICAN BIRD

THE BIG AMERICAN BIRD

THE owner of an Alabama plantation directed me to a field, saying, 'There you will find wild turkeys following the plowman like blackbirds.'

I sat down in the edge of the woods at an end of the plowing. Presently, with a scraping flutter, a twenty-pound gobbler came out of the wood and stalked stiffly into the field. He followed along the freshly turned furrow eating grubs, turning to one side and allowing the negro and his mule to pass within sixty or seventy yards of him. He gobbled when the negro spoke to the mule. A crow flying over cawed, and he again gobbled. When the negro wordily denounced the mule for his stiff-neckedness and general depravity he gobbled vehemently.

A number of other gobblers came out of the woods. One turned aside to run down a grasshopper, but the rest walked with dignified bearing straight for the plowed land. They had burnished bronze suits, dull purple heads and necks, velvety black breasts, and foot-long black beards. They weighed from twelve to twenty pounds.

From behind the fence I watched them with a glass. When they started back to the woods, I tried to avoid being seen. But the leading gobbler, with head towering up like a young giraffe, stopped, looked this way and that, then called 'Put!' All leaped into the air in a second, sweeping about man-high above the field, and sailed over the tree-tops.

I could not help thinking about the shrewdness of these gobblers. Hunted constantly, turkeys are alert and extremely difficult of close approach. They allow no man within gunshot. Yet these birds had mental processes and sufficient daring to discover that this plowman was unarmed.

While I was searching for wild-turkey nests in Texas the suspicious actions of a crow suggested that he too was looking for something. He flew slowly over the tree-tops and watched the earth closely. Suddenly he veered a little for a better look, then — plainly bluffing — flew on a short distance, then circled back and alighted in a treetop.

Here he kept his eyes on a stump in the edge of an outstanding clump of pines. He had discovered a turkey on her nest. Silently, impatiently, he waited for her to leave it. Suddenly he stopped fidgeting.

Evidently the hen was moving. A half-minute later she passed near me in the woods, eagerly picking up food. The crafty crow flew straight to the eggs and had devoured three before my coming put him to flight. There had been fourteen eggs. These the hen had covered with pine-straw before leaving, and the crow had uncovered only those he ate.

The nest was on the ground close to the stump and partly concealed by a drooping pine limb. It was a shallow basin-like depression, thinly lined with grass. It appeared to have been hurriedly made and probably represented the work of only a few minutes. Safety for the eggs requires the turkey hen, in common with other birds, to conceal the nest. Invariably when leaving it she covers the eggs with grass, leaves, or weeds, to conceal them from crows, foxes, and other egg-eating enemies, and man.

Stealthily she leaves her nest when going to feed. Cautiously she returns to it. The eggs usually number between eight and fifteen. Four weeks of incubation are required.

In less than half an hour the hen returned. Finding the broken eggshells, she stretched herself to full height, looking and listening for a minute. After carrying the broken pieces into the pines and scratching leaves over them she resumed her seat upon the nest.

On another occasion, in seating myself on a log to write up notes, a turkey hen which I had not seen was frightened from her nest. This was a rudely scratched depression of the log. She sat with her body parallel to the log. There were seventeen eggs. Some nests are in or by a clump of bushes, weeds, or grass.

Most wild turkeys are hatched during May and June. Of course the vain gobbler never helps incubate the eggs nor assists in rearing the children.

Youngsters and mother remain together until midwinter. The hen whose eggs or youngsters have been destroyed will sometimes join a hen with a family and is allowed to assist in bringing up the brood. If a mother hen is killed, her youngsters, if found by any hen, will be promptly adopted and brought up with all the best wild-turkey traditions.

Wet weather, which so thins the ranks of domestic young turkeys, is also deadly, though less so, with wild broods. Lice and insect pests also take the lives of many a young wild turkey, though here again the domestic species suffers more than the wild.

Many longtime observers have expressed the opinion that the wild-turkey crop is about sixty per cent of the number of eggs laid. If this be correct, it is a higher average than most domestic turkey-raisers attain. The proportion of hens hatched exceeds the number of gobblers. And the conspicuous markings and the revealing gobble greatly increase the life risk of a gobbler over a hen and are another cause of the hens' so greatly outnumbering gobblers. The gobble is heard a mile or farther, and tells every hunter within hearing where turkey may possibly be had.

In most localities there are few gobblers and many hens. On rainy days the peacock-proud gobbler, mad as a wet hen, instead of strutting about and gobbling as usual to let the ladies know where he is, spends a dismal day under cover trying to keep his fine feathers dry. Rain and dress parade do not mix. Rainy weather during gobbling time may result in a slightly decreased turkey crop.

Now and then a gobbler may live an almost solitary life — roost alone, and seek food alone. But the wild turkey likes the company of his kind, and the head of the species is strong for strut and show. During gobbling time — March, April, and May — gobblers and hens flock together.

One spring I followed an old gobbler. I slept near his roosting-tree, which he occupied alone. He gobbled about four o'clock in the morning. Instantly gobblers in every direction answered. Alert and suspicious, he flew to the ground four to five hundred feet distant and again gobbled. Close to this spot he strutted and paraded for two or three hours, occasionally gobbling. Two or three hens came to seek him, but he did not forget danger. He at last spied me and hastened to other parts. That night his roost was with a flock over the water a mile or more from his roost of the preceding night.

The proud and parading gobbler has been a polygamous fellow for generations. At early morn some old fellow gobbles from his tree-top roost.

A MOUNTAIN LAKE

Instantly there is a reply from every gobbler within hearing. In regions of safety this hulla-baloo of tree-top gobbling may continue for half an hour. But in most places the gobblers are becoming cautious and descend to the earth shortly after the first call. Often all the morning long the gobblers strut about, giving a gobble at intervals to let local hens know their whereabouts.

The breast of the gobbler by midwinter or early spring carries a deposit, or reservoir, of fat, which is consumed during the gobbling time, when he is doing too much strutting and parading to search for food. It will be recalled that the sperm whale has literally an oil-reservoir in the top of his head in which is stowed several barrels of sperm oil, which he consumes during periods when he is not hunting food. This food-reservoir in the turkey indicates that for generations the gobbler during the spring has been too busy to eat.

During gobbling, strutting time, gobblers are independent and belligerent. When they fight, others of the flock scamper away. The fight may last two or three hours and commonly ends with the exhaustion of one or the other. Though blood may be shed, neither of the combatants is likely to be even severely injured. Their spurs are short and comparatively harmless. Generally, after pecking and kicking at each other a few times, the gobblers clinch by each getting a grip on each other's featherless necks or heads. Then they pull and push and twist. Rarely is the clinch broken before the fight is over, and during its continuance they may trample over a quarter of an acre of land. In their pulling and hauling each appears to be lifting upward with all his might, as though in hopes of throwing his combatant over his shoulder or of pulling his head off.

The gobbling season over, old gobblers run together and coöperate in a most friendly manner, and rarely do any strutting or gobbling. During summer the hens are with the children, the gobblers by themselves. Late autumn, for a brief period, all may flock together. If food is not plentiful, they wander afar in search of it, and they appear to know where it is most likely to be found. They travel leisurely on foot. As they advance, flock joins flock until an impressive number are together. At a stream they hesitate, if not hungry, collecting along the edge and in the tree-tops. If no log is found, they fly across, some starting from tree-tops, others from the water's edge.

In midwinter the turkeys are commonly in three separate flocks — young gobblers in one, old gobblers in another, and the hens and young ladies together in another. The beard of the young gobbler appears in November. But rarely does a youngster gobble and take on vain airs until more than a year old.

The largest flock of wild turkeys that I have seen was in Northwestern Utah in autumn. There must have been two hundred and fifty. They appeared in excellent health and spirits. More than half were that year's output. Evidently it had been a good local season in wild-turkey world.

At times when all ages and sexes are running together it is likely to be an old hen that leads the flock. They time their movements so as to arrive at that night's roosting-place by sundown. Rarely do they fly. Possibly this would tell news to too many enemies. In case they are behind time, feeding ceases and all go on a run. Arriving at the roosting-place, each flies to its perch.

Sometimes a horned owl will alight on a limb

by a solitary turkey hen, between her and the tree, and edge up to her with a loud, 'Who, who!' The turkey moves away, the owl following and repeating his edging and bullying and shouting until the end of the limb is reached. If the turkey flies the pursuing owl usually catches her before she alights.

Turkeys frequently change their roosting-place. This probably saves them from numerous raids by enemies in fur and feathers and with shotguns. Commonly they have a number of regular roosting-places in their territory and make a change every night or two. They roost two or three on a limb, well up in a tall tree generally, the flock occupying a number of closely assembled trees. Their preference is for trees that stand in or near the water. Probably in these roosts their dreams are less frequently disturbed.

Wild turkeys have a home territory — that is, they live through all seasons year after year, in one locality. Commonly this territory is less than three miles across. If food is plentiful, they travel but little, and this mostly afoot. In some mountainous localities the abundance of food in the lower part of their territory in early spring, and up the slopes in early summer, causes them to follow the food-line, and this amounts to near migration. But, strictly speaking, they are resident and not migratory birds. In times of drought or other food-failures they simply emigrate to new scenes where food shortage is not a problem.

One March I ranged Texas watching turkey ways with a field-glass. Early one morning, by means of a boat, I slipped close up on a flock of thirty or more feeding in the trees. Ravenously they were devouring the spring buds. Local people spoke of it as 'budding.' I heard the turkeys while still a quarter of a mile off. Their heavy bodies were too much for the smaller limbs, and they were almost constantly in motion, fluttering, balancing, or flying. A number that I drifted beneath were flattened out most ungracefully on the limbs with outstretching legs, neck, and wings bearing on the light springy twigs as they reached here and there for the buds. Occasionally one fell through or overboard, and the beating and booming and flopping of wings kept up a constant uproar.

The next day I found this flock of all ages and sexes feeding upon a dry ridge nearly two miles distant. The following afternoon I crawled close up on them while they were feeding along the edge of the extending rising backwater of a stream. Wildly they threw leaves with raking backward scratches, rapidly tearing up the soggy leaves and stirring square rods of surface every few minutes. So definitely were they feeding in a given direction — toward a roosting-place — that one might have trailed them by the 'point' of scratched places. Three or four turkeys were doing sentinel duty. My presence was at first suspected, and then I was seen by a hen on rear guard. She made a warning call. A few seconds later she sounded a definite alarm, and all legged it away through the woods.

When I surprised the flock the next day, about half the number flew, some far away, others alighting in near-by tree-tops. Single file a number ran wildly away into the woods.

Grasshoppers are prime turkey food; those of all ages are eaten — small, soft, hoppy ones, and the fancy-winged, case-hardened ones. If the turkey is exterminated, the insect world will doubtless celebrate and multiply. Every day the turkey consumes wholesale quantities of varieties of grubs and numerous hard-shelled beetles. Soft berries and fruits and many kinds of hard-shelled seeds and at times buds of bushes and trees are taken, these especially during the brief period of swelling buds.

Immediately after eating to fullness it is common for a flock of turkeys to loll and take dust-baths or squat about in sunny places. Sometimes they play. They will spar with one another, chase each other about, do a kind of waltz, and often parade about with wings upraised over their backs.

The habits of wild and tame turkeys are very much alike; in fact any one who is acquainted with the habits of either can pretty accurately judge of the ways of the other. In appearance the wild turkey is trimmer and more slender than the tame one. The tail-band on the domestic species is commonly white, but on the wild ones it is likely to vary. The head of the wild turkey is apt to be bluish or purple, in the tame species reddish. The wild and tame species cross readily, and they and their hybrids sometimes flock together.

One of the most deliciously flavored wild turkeys that I ever tasted had fattened on piñon nuts. Another in the same locality was served me by a prospector. The first bite suggested a salad made up of cedar twigs and cedar oil. This bird evidently had fattened chiefly upon cedar berries.

Many people consider the wild turkey a synonym for indecision, and numerous writers have called the family stupid and witless. True, he has weak streaks. He hesitates and hesitates when not hurried, and a trap with not a particle of camouflage is likely to be alluring. Then, too, he is a stickler for old customs, he is against modern ways; the customs of his parents, even back to the tenth generation, are the ways for his guidance.

But the turkey is no fool. He has decision and sustained watchfulness. One September I lay behind a log in the mountains of southern Arkansas watching a few deer feeding out into an open. A flock of turkeys came over the tree-tops and alighted in the sunny grass before me. The burnished, richly bronzed coats of the gobblers shone in the sunshine. They looked and walked suspiciously about, so that I wondered if they carried a keen nose and had scented me. I watched them with my field-glasses, and I knew that they had not seen me. To test their eyesight and alertness, I raised my hand above the top of the log. Immediately a hen and a gobbler called 'Put! Put!' and 'put' they did. With a whir of wings they were instantly going. With rapid leg-work they vanished into the woods.

The turkey has some mental processes or he would hardly take advantage of the feasts uncovered by unarmed plowmen and use sentinels when feeding where the hunter is at large. It may be only instinct that causes the turkey to seek our acid ash-piles and pungent, active ant-hills in the woods for effective dust spray against insects; but wild turkeys are not witless.

The fundamentals used by a successful wild-turkey hunter would enable him to bag any big wild game. I have never killed a wild turkey. But I am certain that the hunter who returns thankfully laden from a wild-turkey hunt may well be doubly thankful, for his feet, lungs, eyes, and wits will have been exactingly used and bettered.

Many times I have hunted the wild turkey with a double-barreled field-glass. This was about

as exacting and exciting as hunting the grizzly
and the bighorn with the same equipment. Getting within short range required knowledge of
their territory and their customs and stalking.
Random rambles rarely showed them even at
long range. Many a flock on which I was trying
my woodcraft, planning to make long and close
observations of their ways, added to my outdoor
lore by failing to coöperate. They left me in possession of the other side of the field.

I went with a skillful turkey-hunter who had
tried for a large gobbler through seven years. In
this time he had bagged a number of other gobblers and hens. We rose early, tramped miles, hid,
used a turkey-call, ran on detours to likely places,
and stalked.

Several times we heard the swish and roar of
this old gobbler's escaping wings; two or three
times we saw his running legs beneath the far-off
pines; and once, with a telescope, we had a brief
look at him and his crowd.

One sunny afternoon, when close to the gobbler, the hunter went through a varied lot of calls
which were intelligently intended to rouse the
gobbler's curiosity or to challenge him. Then the

hunter remained silent. We sat near each other with backs against the base of a large pine. Sunlight and shadow were upon the forest floor. We heard footsteps of turkey approaching cautiously.

Instead of the old fellow there were several young gobblers. Two walked along a log a dozen feet from us. On spying us they stopped and looked. They stretched out their necks and looked again. One came close and eyed me curiously. He moved his head from side to side in a puzzled manner. He seemed to be thinking, 'This is the spot where that call came from, but this is no gobbler.' He leaned toward me with his weight on one foot as though to kick forward with the other foot, like a kangaroo. Had he made the slightest movement, I should have dodged. But he moved slowly away with the others, all talking in low tones to themselves.

In leaving the woods we came close upon a flock, mostly hybrids. This the hunter attributed to the wild hens' crossing with near-by tame gobblers, because of a local scarcity of wild gobblers.

The wild turkey has managed to survive numerous wide-awake enemies, and has succeeded in this because of his native shrewdness and the ability to be alert and cautious at times when precautions are needed.

Man hunts the turkey with traps, nets, dogs, and guns; wolves, foxes, lions, cats, owls, crows, snakes, and insects by the million prey upon turkey; but over two million square miles or more this bronze fellow still has a place in the sun.

The turkey survives in greater or less numbers in a dozen or more States. He is even plentiful in a number of localities in New Mexico, Texas, Arkansas, Alabama, Florida, and Mexico. His ranks are thinning, his territory is diminishing, and he is in danger of extermination. Hunters are increasing, and the sheltered regions in which he can find food and hiding are becoming fewer and smaller. Yet, such is the virility of this bird, moderate protective legislation and education would not only save him but perhaps enable him to multiply. Legislation against trapping is the chief need. And this, together with a few refuges, would save him.

Originally the wild turkey was widely distributed. It was found all over the United States, except in the extreme northwestern part, and abounded in regions of old Mexico. Audubon speaks of buying wild turkeys in Boston markets, and says that full-grown ones in Kentucky markets often sold for ten cents or less. I had seen the wild turkey in southern Ohio, in Florida, and in Kansas, but had forgotten about him. When I commenced exploring northern Arizona, I expected first of all to see a big grizzly bear, a desert coyote, or some such distinctive life and color. But the first wild life was a wild-turkey hen which dashed by pursuing a grasshopper. From the edge of the woods I watched a near-by flock of twenty or more of all ages, which were rushing, grabbing, and turning this way and that as they effectively fed upon the excited, high-jumping hoppers.

No one appears to know just how long a wild turkey may live. A few have been watched for ten years, and it is likely that they may live twice as long. If a turkey survives the insects, the wet weather, and the devouring enemies which beset it during the first year of its life, and does not meet with violent death, it is likely to live to a ripe old age. The turkey is the weightiest, biggest American bird, weighing from ten to forty pounds, according to his chances.

The turkey appears to have started in life as an American. His bones are exhibited in American fossil deposits eons old. He was a wild, prehistoric American. His bones have been found beneath the ruins of cliff houses untold centuries of age, and what appears to have been roosting-places for domestic turkeys were attached to both pueblos and cliff houses. The American Indian domesticated the turkey ages ago.

About four hundred years ago the Spaniards in conquering Mexico found turkeys both wild and domestic. Domestic turkeys were shipped to Spain, and in a few years the gobble of the turkey would be heard all over Europe. Then this American bird commenced to play his part in world affairs. Europeans at first mistook him for a species of African guinea, and he was misnamed. His pride and plumage also caused many to think he surely must be a worthy fellow of the peacock family.

Four hundred years of American turkey history, wild and domestic, is adventurous, exciting, and progressive enough to make good reading. The turkey has a visible place in literature and art; many a printed page he has inspired, and his story has brought to our attention some of the curious customs of our broad-brimmed ancestors.

The New England settlers, it is said, fell upon their knees, then upon the aborigines. They also found time to fall upon wild turkeys. Generations ago the turkey went close to the heart of white folks, and even to this day rivals the 'possum' in power to stir deeply the internal feelings of the colored folks. So definite and sustained is the longing for this bird that it is doubtful if any other has caused so many raids in the dark or encouraged such audacious profiteering. Turkey association with all kinds of people in our country makes him all-American and democratic to the heart.

For turkey — the big American bird of beard and bronze — there are no substitutes just as good.

We are thankful in our hearts for turkey traditions. The turkey is united and inseparable with Christmas and Thanksgiving, and is almost certain to be among those present on every festive occasion. He figures in high living. He ever roosts high, but is preyed upon, caught, cornered, and prayed over.

He associates with pie, piety, and prayers. When the Harvest Home is celebrated, his bright and bronzed feathers often mingle with autumn's colored and flying leaves, and scenes where he roosted hear him gobble no more.

WITH FAMOUS TRAVELERS

WITH FAMOUS TRAVELERS

BIRDS know no boundary lines and sing to the hearts of all people.

Each spring with the coming of the flowers, while the trees are putting on leaf and bloom, the birds come back to their summer homes. Quietly, eagerly they overspread North America. The bobolinks nest over a large area around the Great Lakes. The redstart nests in the northern United States and over most of Canada, from the Atlantic to the Pacific. The hermit thrush sings his famous song over nearly all the north woods. Then millions of nests and more millions of children.

As a boy I had the idea that all birds wintered somewhere in the South and that in summer all went an equal distance northward. As a matter of fact, not all migrating birds fly South in winter. In mountainous districts some birds get a decided change of climate by moving from the upper mountain-slopes to the foothills or to the plains.

But twice each year, the strange vast movements of migration call the birds of entire nations to leave accustomed scenes and travel far away.

Off to another continent they go, scarcely an individual of a migratory species remaining behind. This exodus includes more than four hundred nations of birds, each numbering millions. Birds that have both a summer and a winter home, that shift and swing up and down the earth, north and south with the seasons, may spend half_or more of each year in migration. It is probable that birds, in their ordinary traveling in quest of food and for pure frolic, cover more miles daily than the average person covers in a year.

The golden plover is perhaps the greatest of bird travelers. It has a yearly migration-route of twenty thousand miles in the form of an ellipse about eight thousand miles long and two thousand miles across, breeding within the Arctic Circle and migrating to Patagonia.

About the first of March the plovers move northward in flocks, in a northeasterly direction across South America. Reaching the coast of Louisiana or Texas, they fly slowly up the Mississippi valley, across central Canada. By the first of June they reach their nesting-grounds beyond timber-line within the Arctic Circle.

The golden plover is a graceful, handsome bird

A FORESTED CAÑON BELOW TIMBER-LINE IN THE ROCKIES

in holiday dress. He is golden and blackish above, with yellowish tail, black breast, and a whitish margin line separating the colors of back and breast. Often in the tundras or moorlands he will stand, looking like a beautiful statuette, and there give his winning, plaintive, and pleasing love song. For a few seconds he waits silent before giving it again. Then it is repeated, perhaps a score of times without moving.

As soon as the young are able to fly, all move eastward to Labrador and Nova Scotia to feed upon the crowberries. They grow plump almost to bursting, and their very flesh is stained red with the juice of the berries they have eaten.

From Nova Scotia the plovers make a remarkable flight southward. Leaving the Atlantic coast, if the weather is fair, they make the 2400-mile dash without stopping, and alight near the mouth of the Orinoco River in South America, having averaged fifty miles an hour, day and night, for forty-eight hours.

About the first of October these birds, old and young, leave the northern coast of South America and go southward to the Argentine Republic for a vacation. Here the resident South American birds are busy bringing up families, but the plover, having nested in the far northland, spends this summer in picnicking.

This yearly round of the golden plover is a romantic one. He has a fair knowledge of North and South America and is acquainted with the topography of several nations. He knows intimately the strange Arctic moorland, and something of the sea, of high mountains, great forests, the mighty Amazon, the rivers of North America, its Great Lakes, and its far-stretching plains.

The golden plover of America and the plover of the Hawaiian Islands and Siberia are practically identical in appearance and habits. In summer their ranges bring them within one hundred miles of contact, yet it is doubtful if they ever see each other. From Alaska the Pacific plovers have a long flight of more than two thousand miles across the wide, islandless sea to their winter home in the Hawaiian Islands. The black-bellied plover makes its summer home along the shores of the Arctic Ocean of North America, Russia, and Siberia. It winters in South America, Africa, India, and Australia.

Around the Arctic Circle in early June the days

are almost stormless and the midnight sun shines through all the hours. Here are millions of merry birds, scores of varieties. They crowd the wide tundras and fill the realm of stunted trees where the forest makes its frontier stand in the farthest north. They are animated, active, and songful, in the midst of courtship or enjoying the honeymoon. It is a land of loveliness.

Males of many varieties, in their loveliest finery, parade and pose, strut and race, perform and sing. They are trying to win a mate or to please one they have won. Bird love mounts high. There is an extraordinary exhibition of wooings. Robins sing their well-known song; geese make their favorite sounds; gulls and terns give expression to their joy; white-crowned and golden-crowned sparrows are happy; sandpipers and plovers are musical; the willow ptarmigan are hurling themselves into the air, crowing and challenging. Even the ducks become musical. The tiny ruby-crowned kinglet, restless as a wren, exposes his red crest and stirs the air with a loud, clear soprano song. The Lapland longspur is one of the most enthusiastic and animated of these singers.

The northern phalarope is here. In this case it

is the lady who is the larger, who wears the finery and does the parading and courting. The male, in a subdued suit, is at first stoically indifferent to her attentions. She shows her finery and glides near him as he sits indifferently in the water. She comes closer. He turns aside and pretends to search for food. She circles him again, arching her neck and bowing her head. He turns away. At last he flees to another pool. The gentle wooer follows. There is no escape. He accepts her and also the task of brooding the eggs while she swims idly and gracefully about. The beautiful youngsters are in buff and brown.

The northern phalarope migrates to Guatemala. Birds that nest in the north never nest while in their winter homes, though many of them are in this summer climate during the heyday of the nesting-time of the resident birds.

In all the love-making on the wild, strange Arctic tundra there is no courtship more romantic and charming than that of the Western sandpiper, that migrates from Central and South America. These little birds are gentle and confiding. They trip daintily about upon the moss and through the tufted grass. He runs to and fro before her, showing his graceful form to best advantage. She has a soft call of 'weet-weet.' She modestly avoids him, but he grows more energetic and aggressive and pompously struts before her like a turkey, dragging his wings and spreading his tail. He puts forth his best efforts.

Finally he leaps into the air. Poising and hovering in one spot for a minute or longer, he pours forth a plaintive and intense song. Then, extending his wings above his back, he settles slowly, uttering a more hopeful song as he comes to the grass beside her. He continues with happy twittering notes. She makes him a devoted, courageous, motherly mate.

A bird whose flight is puzzling many a naturalist is the red-eyed vireo. It winters in Central America. It appears each spring at the mouth of the Mississippi, traveling about twenty miles a day. It proceeds at this leisurely rate until it reaches northern Nebraska; then, suddenly, in the space of twenty-four hours, it appears in British Columbia, a thousand miles to the north. This interesting performance is repeated by them year after year. It nests across the continent, from Nova Scotia to Vancouver Island.

The cliff swallows and the black-poll warblers have winter homes in the same territory in northern South America. The migration habits of these two species, however, are strangely unlike.

The swallows start northward early, choose the longest way, and journey leisurely. They travel only during the day, lying over each night. They start about the first of March and travel westward across South and Central America, around the west shore of the Gulf of Mexico, then eastward up the Mississippi and Ohio valleys, and thence northeast to Nova Scotia. They average less than thirty miles a day and arrive in Nova Scotia on about the same date each year.

The black-poll warblers travel only at night, go at high speed, choose the shortest way, and wait until the latest moment before starting for their summer home. They fly across the Caribbean Sea to Cuba, and for nearly seven thousand miles, above sea, lakes, rivers, and mountains to Alaska, they follow a straight line.

They make the journey in about a month, averaging about two hundred miles every twenty-four hours, and sometimes making several hundred miles in a single night. They arrive in

Alaska late in May. This is, perhaps, the most numerous species of warbler, and they scatter over a summer range about three thousand miles wide and along a north-and-south line more than a thousand miles in length.

In the van of the spring migration, which starts in February, flies the Canada goose, closely followed by ducks, robins, bluebirds, and blackbirds. It would be pleasant to think that ducks and geese are sent as advance messengers of the sun to tell us that summer, with its long, bright days, its birds and flowers, is coming — is already driving winter away; while the robins might be considered as personally conducting spring back to us. The robin appears to advance into the north on the very wave of spring, occasionally a day in advance or behind this warm flood. At first this advance is slow, the robin and the wave making only a few miles a day. Then the movement becomes faster, and during the last few days of their journey robins that go to the Far North may travel seventy miles or more daily.

The high tide of the migratory movement is reached, perhaps, early in May. But the majority of species stay in their warm southern home till spring is well advanced in the territory through which they will travel; so the season will be well begun when they arrive in summer nesting-scenes. Last of all, about the first of June, come the warblers and thrushes.

Birds that start early and do not go very far north spend weeks picnicking before a nest is built. But a number of species that nest in and close to the Barren Lands or the far north shores of North America must spend so much time going to and from the summer home that many do their courting along the way and begin nest-building immediately after their arrival.

The majority of migrant birds are night travelers. These include all the great families of thrushes, flycatchers, warblers, and orioles, most of the sparrows, and the shore-birds. They usually start immediately after dark and stop just before dawn. It is probable that they choose this time because the night gives greater security from winged enemies and man. Some species travel day and night.

Among the day travelers are hawks, swallows, nighthawks, the chimney swift, hummingbirds, waxwings, crossbills, robins, and bluebirds. Most of these day travelers combine food-hunting with travel and commonly make only a short distance each day.

In a few species, we know, the flock follows a leader, and it may be that this habit is general. In most cases the birds travel in flocks, with the males a week or so in advance of the females. The red-winged blackbird and the males of many other species, reaching the probable nesting-scenes, at once begin singing so as to attract the ladies who shall be first to arrive, although these are not due for a week or two.

Species differ widely in their traveling habits. Some move forward in speedy flight and may cover several hundred or a thousand miles in a single flight of less than twenty-four hours. After such a flight they commonly lie by to rest and feed for a few days. Many kinds of birds that winter in Central America make the long flight across the Gulf of Mexico, a distance of from four hundred to seven hundred miles. A few species may cover a thousand miles a day and gain the summer nesting-grounds in a remarkably short time.

Other birds travel by easy stages, going only

twenty or thirty miles a day. Very few average
more than one hundred miles a day. They enjoy
the journey as they go, lead a jolly life, and grow
fat on the way. The average distance traveled
by all migrating birds from New Orleans to Minnesota is about twenty-three miles per day, but
after passing Minnesota many that have traveled
somewhat leisurely increase their speed and ofttimes double it. One species of warbler spends
thirty days traveling the first one thousand miles
and in the next fifteen days covers twenty-five
hundred miles.

Many kinds of birds spend the summer in northern United States regions and winter in the
Southern States. Of those that summer in Canada and Alaska, some winter in the United States
and others in Central and South America or near
the Antarctic. Thus, some birds see the United
States only as travelers; others are residents and do
not travel at all. So we have permanent residents,
summer residents, winter residents, and visitors.

The American crossbill is a gypsy among birds.
It does not migrate at a regular time, nor follow
a regular route, nor nest regularly in a locality.
The crossbills are more like wanderers than any

other species that I know. They may turn up almost anywhere. Where food is abundant, they make long stays. They usually travel in small flocks and feed in forests. Evidently they travel about for pleasure and without any prearranged route.

The selection of the migration-route is determined by the food-supply. There must be places along the way where this supply is certain. It does not much matter how widely separated these feeding-places are, nor even if a side journey is necessary. The different kinds of food that different species require, and the habit of some birds of traveling at night and that of others of traveling in the daytime, are factors which have probably helped to determine the well-known migration-routes.

Do you wonder how birds find the way, how day after day or night after night they follow a given course, traveling thousands of miles through the air, as if following a line of guideposts in the sky? A majority of all northward migration probably is confined to four well-known routes. It is true that even at night birds can see landmarks, and that they sometimes follow river valleys, but often they travel rapidly when nothing can be seen or heard to direct their course. Evidently they have a sixth sense — a sense of direction.

Birds in closed cages, or while stupefied by chloroform, have been carried miles from home into regions where they never were before. When released, they promptly and apparently without effort, returned home.

Usually, through storm or cloud, as straight as a crow flies, birds make their way to the desired point. But birds of almost every species sometimes become confused, lose their sense of direction, and fly about in a bewildered manner. More than once I have seen flocks of birds traveling rapidly in just the opposite direction to that they evidently thought they were going.

Each migration is filled with romance and adventure such as a long journey across sea and land is sure to give. A few species go northward over one route and for the southward journey follow an entirely different air trail. The golden plover is one of the famous travelers who returns South over a route far removed from the one taken into the North. But other birds also take unusual migratory routes southward.

The Connecticut, or tamarack, warbler goes northward up the Mississippi valley. He nests in northern Canada. So far as known, only one of his nests has ever been discovered, though these birds are numbered by the million. On the journey south they first go eastward to the Atlantic, then pass down along the coast to their winter home.

The marbled godwit nests in North Dakota and southern Canada. When time for autumn migration arrives, one flock of these birds flies to the Atlantic Ocean, another west across the mountains to the Pacific. Then both move southward along the coast and unite for the winter in Central America.

The Ross snow goose makes an interesting migratory journey. From the summer home at the mouth of the Mackenzie River in the Far North, it flies southward to about the northern line of the United States, then turns westward, crosses the mountains, goes southward along the coast, and winters in southern California.

The northern route of the Western tanager is somewhat out of the ordinary in bird migrations. From Guatemala they move northward and they enter the United States in Arizona and New Mexico. Here they appear to divide, one section traveling northward as far as central Colorado, while the other moves westward to the Pacific and up along the coast to near the northern line of the United States, then turns eastward and crosses the mountains, a number flying southeast and a few perhaps ultimately reaching northern Colorado.

What a marvelous procession these migrating birds make!

In 1808 Alexander Wilson, the ornithologist, for four hours carefully observed passenger pigeons traveling north. Within that time, as he estimated, he saw at least two billion of them pass! Late in April two or three hundred species of birds, each numbering from one million to many millions, are on the wing. Countless flocks are in procession for thousands of miles along the main migration-traveled route. In a short time and in an orderly manner, millions of birds arrive and become settlers for the summer.

Many of these birds are famous color-bearers. The scarlet tanager in black and scarlet, the brilliant Baltimore oriole, the redstart — 'the little torch' — the rose-breasted grosbeak, the Arkansas goldfinch, and many others are dressed in bright and gorgeous hues. The bobolink wears black and white while journeying to the northland, but before leaving for his winter home puts on a suit of buff and olive; while the scarlet tanager in autumn is clad in greenish yellow.

Many dangers are encountered by these traveling birds. They are drowned in the Great Lakes or in the Gulf of Mexico. Violent storms occasionally overwhelm them. Hundreds have been known to perish in a single storm, and many thousands in the course of one migratory season. Sometimes they starve for lack of food, and gunners lie in wait at many places where they may alight to feed. Until recently the earth all along the way simply bristled with guns.

The test which migration imposes may after all be beneficial. It certainly eliminates the dull-witted and the weak. Sickly birds cannot survive the journey. Each bird must be vigorous, eternally vigilant, and must find its own living along the way.

The migratory habits of the birds of the Eastern Hemisphere are similar to those of the Western.

A number of species from the Pacific Islands and Siberia come to Alaska for the summer. The wheatear of Greenland goes to Africa for the winter. Many European birds spend their winters in Africa.

In the tropics there are a few hundred varieties of resident hummingbirds. How did it happen that not many became migrants? East of the Mississippi there is only the beautiful ruby-throat; in the West probably a dozen varieties. The hummingbirds of the Western mountains, who have as summer neighbors wolves, mountain sheep, and grizzly bears, live in the winter in the midst of parrots, monkeys, and tropical vegetation. The broad-tailed and the rufous are often seen in the Rocky Mountains. The rufous is but a mite, scarcely larger than an insect. Yet this brave little fellow goes all the way over forests and mountains, deserts and plains, and in far-off Alaska builds its artistic lichen decorated nest.

The high mountains in the West prevent the great north-and-south sweep and flow of bird migration which prevails over the eastern half of the United States. The bobolink appears recently

Photograph by P. A. Smoll

THE BROAD-TAILED HUMMINGBIRD

to have developed a route across the Rocky Mountains into Utah, and it may be that other routes are being developed. Bird-life in the mountains of the West is increasing. This probably is due chiefly to increased food-supplies brought by settlement and irrigation.

It may be that these mountains have not been completely explored by a number of species that are yet to inhabit them. Birds are explorers. When there is time after nesting is over, numbers of species explore the country, sometimes for hundreds of miles to the west, north, and east of their summer nesting-places. A number of species, as soon as the young are able to fly, explore the territory to the north of their summer home before starting southward. Among these are the herons and robins. They probably do this simply for food or for a lark, but they may be seeking a new home for themselves or their children for the coming year.

The question is often asked, but I believe has never been entirely satisfactorily answered, 'Why do birds move from north to south each year?'

It is undoubtedly for the advantages of migration, and possibly, too, because of a little of the gypsy spirit that is in them, the love of change.

Most birds and animals seek seclusion during the time they are bringing up their young. In many cases the territory occupied by the birds in summer is many times the size of their winter territory. Many species in summer spread over two thirds of the North American continent.

Then, too, the climate of the earth has changed. It may be that the ancestors of many of these migrating birds lived in the North before they were driven by the glacial epoch into the South. They use the opportunity that spring affords to make this old home an annual visit. Those as-yet-unread secrets of geology may sometime reveal the history, the origin, and the development of bird migration.

Though we do not know the causes behind bird migration, many things of interest concerning it are now understood. We know where many of the birds winter, when they start northward, the route they travel, how fast they go, when they arrive at their destination, where they spend the summer, and the time they will start on their southern journey.

But there are many things of interest which

have not yet been discovered. Perhaps the airplane will advance our knowledge of these other fliers.

The route of the arctic tern has not as yet been discovered. In fact but little is known concerning its traveling habits. It summers near the Arctic Circle and winters in Antarctic regions. The distance between the two is eleven thousand miles!

In going from one to the other the bird makes a journey that is almost equal to a half-circuit of the earth. When the terns arrive at their Arctic summer home the midnight sun is in the sky, and during the two months' time that they stay they have no sunset. It is the 'Great Day' of the Arctic summer. For two months of the time they are in the Antarctic the sun is ever in sight, unless the sky be hidden by clouds, and during the remainder of the time that they are there it dips such a short distance below the horizon that daylight does not end. No other bird or being that we know of has so much sunshine, or so much daylight, as the arctic tern.

Another mystifying migration is that of the chimney swift, which utterly disappears for a few months each year. The movements of these birds can easily be followed each autumn, as they move southward near the Atlantic coast, from New York and New England, and in countless flocks gather at the Gulf of Mexico. Suddenly they disappear. One day they are there by the thousands, and the next day they are not to be seen. No one knows where they winter.

Five months later they reappear at the Gulf where last seen and start northward for their summer home. This mysterious disappearance has caused many strange stories to be told concerning them. In times past the story was current that they dived into the mud and hibernated through the winter. Where they go is one of the thousands of unanswered questions in bird world; but it is quite probable that they winter somewhere in the secluded forests of northern South America or southern Mexico.

The average length of the birds' summer stay is about three months. Those species which have gone only a thousand miles north from their winter home start south early in the summer, sometimes by the first of July, but most of them not until a month or six weeks later. A few species remain until forced south by cold and food-shortage; these may have six months or more in the summer home.

Early in August over the northern half of the United States a number of the summer birds are leaving, or preparing to leave, for the south; at the same time numbers of species that nested farther north are arriving for the winter. Next spring these winter visitors will leave for the north about the time the summer people from the south begin to arrive.

Apparently most birds make something of a prolonged picnic of the entire migratory journey. It may be that while they are collecting in flocks before migrating from their northern summer home, the youngsters gather around some old bird to hear of the adventurous experiences, the exciting times, the strange food and new good things to eat, the wonderful country, and in fact all the other things that are likely to interest the young and inexperienced who have inherited a taste for travel and adventure and are about to make a long journey.

The migration instinct or habit leading birds to start southward at the given time appears as strong in autumn as the call in spring to go northward. For hours — sometimes for a day or two — before starting south, the birds collect in flocks and with some show of excitement chatter away. I have read of ducks, captured when young and kept with clipped wings, in the first autumn of their lives when the day came to migrate, being unable to fly, set off for the South on foot.

A bird traveling to and fro between his summer and winter homes looks upon the outspread world. He sees rivers that wind between forested banks, and the silver and tangled lines of countless streams, all shimmering in the sun. He passes over lakes that reflect the cloud and the blue, over fields of green and gold, over ragged groves, grassy fields, dark forests, rolling hills, and rugged mountains. He knows all weather, has storm and sunshine, sees sunsets, and all the cloud scenery of the sky. In spring the earth is fresh and green. In autumn it lies in sunshine, a wonderland of color. Sometimes its uneven surface is overlaid with whitest snow.

The migrations, the adventurous travels of billions of birds constitute one of the foremost wonders of this wonder-filled world. The journeys of the birds up and down the earth, from summer nesting-places where the children are born and reared to the warm, luxurious southland, where all spend a jolly vacation in the very heart of summer; the dangers and courtships along the thousands of miles of travel; the adventures they meet; the hunters they escape twice each year; the multitude of those that start on this wonderful journey and lose their lives on the way; the strange people and places the migrants visit; the picnics they have among the forests, lakes, and streams where they stop for breakfast, lunch, or dinner; the flags of different nations flying — these are a few of the never-ending sights and experiences of the travelers in their adventurous travels between the flower-filled land of the midnight sun and the tropic scenes where green summer ever lives and white winter never comes.

These things are educational, and bird migration arouses the imagination, stirs the mind into thinking, and gives material for reflection and romance.

THE END